Making
Life
Meaningful

Making Life Meaningful

Joseph Stein

Nelson-Hall, Chicago

Library of Congress Cataloging in Publication Data

Stein, Joseph,
   Making life meaningful.

   Includes index.
   1. Social isolation. 2. Alienation (Social
psychology). 3. Interpersonal relations. 4. Psychotherapy. I. Title.
HM291.S8177   301.11'3   78-15347
ISBN 0-88229-375-3

Manufactured in the United States of America

10 9 8 7 6 5 4 3 2 1

Contents

Introduction

Today, more than ever, many people are asking: What am I living for? What meaning does my life have? Such questions reflect people's anxiety and depression, sapping their energy, purpose, and zest for living. Is their negative outlook rooted entirely within themselves, or are they responding to external factors, too? Certainly life often seems absurd, without purpose, at the mercy of chance. Nor can we ignore the man-made ills of a polluted environment, crime, corrupt government, war, and the nuclear menace. Nevertheless, *it is up to each individual to make his or her life significant.*

Meaningful experience does not come ready-made—people must *create* it. They must define clearly those behaviors that enable them to do this and learn to pursue them skillfully. Avoiding superficial advice and oversimplified solutions, this book tries to stimulate the reader to look within, to modify his or her personality in order to release the unique potential for meaningful living present in us all.

The book combines several points of view. I believe this approach will be especially valuable to the contemporary reader because it brings traditional insights and current outlooks together in a manner that allows the reader to use the best of both in his or her daily life.

Meaningful living depends on having a realistic and positive attitude towards oneself. It depends on sound values. It calls for the capacity to form and sustain close relationships. It is important that people feel they are valued

1

members of a circle of friends. They must be absorbed in their everyday, ongoing activity. They must have realistic goals toward which to work and be able to sustain the hope that they will reach them.

In recent years it has become clear that emotional problems are not illnesses. Rather, they are ineffective patterns of behavior that have been learned. Once a person realizes this, he or she is more likely to raise questions and break away from early patterns of behavior that have become frustrating.

Human beings may feel very alone in the world and weighed down by anxiety and boredom. They may be unable to make even the smallest decision without undue stress. They may find it difficult to communicate with those they are close to. Their lack of awareness of who they are and what their goals are is frustrating. A concern with achievement, status, and money may consume their thoughts and energies so that they have little left for personal relationships. An inability to be real and natural may block interaction with others. And they may find, despite their wish to the contrary, that they have no more than a limited capacity to love those who are most important to them.

For the reader who wants to consult a professional person for help with such problems, Chapter 12 presents eleven current approaches to psychotherapy. Each is illustrated with dialogue that brings out its main techniques. This dialogue is real—from actual sessions—selected because many portions of it are representative of what is said generally. But this book is not primarily about psychotherapy; it is about what an individual can do to make life meaningful.

Part One

Meaning
and
Aloneness

Chapter 1

The Person Feels Alone

It is the nature of people, inevitable as drawing breath, to feel alone in the world. Yet, frequently they suffer intensely from their aloneness, especially when deprived of contact with those who are important to them or when they no longer can sustain hope for a brighter future. Consider, for example, Mary and Bill:

Bill has begun to realize that his life is coming to nothing. A relentless fear gnaws at him, whispering that he is not much of a man by any standard—physical, sexual, or as a husband and father. Dare he talk to Mary about these feelings? Even if she listened, could he expect her to understand? She might not care enough about him even to try, and then he would feel utterly humiliated. So, unconsciously, he wears his armor when with her, and their encounters are like battles.

And what of Mary's sense of aloneness? Her deepest

feelings remain buried beneath a dull, perpetual aching. Occasionally she finds flimsy relief in fantasy, glimpsing some part of these feelings. But she never can really know her best self until it flows toward another—until it is shared. Yet she is afraid to reveal herself to Bill. He would try to close himself off, dodging her groping efforts to reach him. Were he to let her in, he would have to confront himself, too. And Mary knows this would be as difficult for him as for her, although he wants desperately to do so. Bitterly, she realizes that her life has little meaning when she is alone.

Even though human beings have a strong need to be known intimately and to share deeply in others, they also have a strong fear of closeness. Closeness leaves them open to a great sense of loss through accident, illness, divorce, infidelity, and death. But by far the greatest danger of losing their partner in a relationship arises from their own immaturity, which prevents them from fulfilling their partners' needs.

Even when people are involved in a close relationship, it is their nature to be so centered in themselves that they cannot share in another as fully as they wish. Nor can they allow themselves to be fully shared. They can never entirely understand or be understood.

They are pulled in too many directions to devote themselves as fully to their loved ones as they might wish. Often they are torn between opposites—a need to explore various people intimately and a training in fidelity. They can never follow one course or the other without wishing they were doing or being something other than what they are. Yet their whole being hungers for completion through union with another. *When they create meaning in this way they feel that their life has been worthwhile.*

The aloneness that always hovers over human beings tends to increase with age. And in the end, when we die, we make a lone voyage, taking no person or thing with us.

Is this aloneness the person's basic state? Or is it natural for him or her to feel a joy in life, which is lost only in adversity? It appears that both aloneness and joy are natural states. The challenge for us all is to combat the aloneness so that we can experience the zest of living. Ideas on how to do this successfully are offered in later chapters.

People who become extremely aware of how alone they are may withdraw from others and from situations that formerly helped make their life meaningful. The once familiar and comfortable people and situations become strange and unreal, resulting in little or no sense of belonging. They squash so many of their thoughts and feelings that, eventually, they can hardly be certain what their real thoughts and feelings are. Their behavior no longer seems to be their own. They stand back and regard it as if it were being performed by somebody else. They have become *alienated*.

Mary expresses some of this sense of alienation from life and people:

What makes me want to isolate myself so much? I want to hide from people, even those who are close—close—to me. I don't want them to know how alone I really feel. When I feel this way, it wears me down until I have no energy, only this enormous fatigue, so that I don't want to do anything at all. What a terrible way to live! This beautiful day—I should be enjoying it! Where do I look for ways to change? How will I ever have the courage to live my life well?

In an effort to escape this growing sense of alienation, people may become absorbed in their work. This is not to say, though, that this increases their feelings of adequacy. Nor do they necessarily feel that they are engaged in meaningful activity. They merely busy themselves with work that fails to offset the growing numbness with which they confront life. Soon they are lost to those who should be important to them; work has become anesthesia for their separateness. They feel utterly empty and cannot take part in anything but their work. Lacking zest and spontaneity, they wonder what it must be like to feel really alive. They resent the wasting of the years; yet they cannot seem to infuse them with meaning.

Hoping to overcome the dead feeling within, they may turn to drugs. They do so not only to feel life within but also to mingle with people again. They even hope that drugs will open them to a close relationship. Drugs usually do weaken the habitual restraint people place on themselves. But instead of opening them to others, drugs often spin a cocoon of fantasy in which they further lose touch with themselves. They may *feel*, but they remain trapped in their private worlds.

Alienated people cannot create meaning out of what they perceive to be the absurdity of life. Meaningful reality has become a drab fantasy to them; so they lose purpose. Of what use, they ask, is purpose in a meaningless world?

Still, many people who are disillusioned by the "absurdity" of life do not withdraw from those about them. Their disillusionment can be understood best through certain historical events. Two world wars within twenty-five years and an ever-present nuclear threat have brought them to a rather grim outlook on life. The brutalities of the concentration camps and the atomic annihilation of Hiroshima contributed to this reaction. They were shocked out of their beliefs in God, goodness, justice, and the steady progression of man toward a better self.

Perhaps those who are disillusioned have adopted a world outlook that is too grim. Perhaps they can once again integrate themselves meaningfully into a world of values, reason, and dignity. Perhaps. But they cannot do this through illusion or by playing games with themselves. If meaning is to sustain them, it cannot be built upon the sands of illusion. Yet once they abandon illusion, they somehow must be able to create a new meaning strong enough to forestall alienation.

To avoid anxiety in a given situation, people may distort what is taking place. Though they do not realize it, they allow themselves to see only what enables them to maintain a favorable picture of themselves. The more their anxiety causes them to see things in their own particular way, the more it contributes to their feeling of being isolated and alone.

People who are insecure may be quite guarded, hostile, and cold. They communicate poorly. They are unrealistic and may really believe that their life will fall to pieces at any moment. They are convinced that the front that they project in order to appear adequate can be seen through; then others would want little or nothing to do with them. They cannot believe that they are likable people whom others want to have around.

Such individuals feel separate from others and actually become so. They develop a two-sided personality. Inwardly they respond one way, while outwardly they try to be acceptable to others. But the careful observer will detect the conflict between their actual reactions and those that they pretend to have. At times, when the mask falls away, they can no longer hide their true response.

Sometimes the way people see things may not be distorted so much as it is simply different. But the result is still that they are not in tune with how others see things. This is more likely to be the case when they mature more rapidly than those about them. Their very development separates them from those with whom they used to be most at ease. They are likely to feel isolated, failing to enjoy a sense of belonging in any group. This failure to belong may occur even when they are secure in a warm family life. Their anxiety is increased, to be relieved only when they move on to new relationships and activities that enable them to be more fully the kinds of people into which they have grown. Then they find a new sense of belonging through their new roles, values, responsibilities, goals, and relationships.

The cold impersonality of urban life can also give rise to feelings of apartness from others. In such an environment people often are actually known to very few others. Nothing illustrates this better than the following situation:

Living in an apartment house in a large city, the person descends in the elevator at the same time every morning on his way to work. The occupant of another apartment regularly descends at the same time, also on his way to work. Yet never once does either recognize the presence of the other and greet him. Instead, each stares straight ahead in the small elevator as if the other did not exist. God forbid that one of them should burp! He would confront the momentous decision of acknowledging the other person by having to say, "Excuse me!"

Adding to the impersonality of the large city is the high rate at which people move about today. They seldom live and die in the same house. They not only move within the city as the needs of their families change, but they also move across country. They are lured by jobs and more desirable living conditions. The more mobile way of life often increases their isolation. A recent study of the moving patterns of employees of large companies indicates there is growing resistance to being transplanted every couple of years.

Because our society changes so rapidly, the generation gap is still with us. Certainly the conflict between our youth and the older generation, though not as intense as it was a decade ago, is still sharp. Many of our youth do not respect their elders because of the cynical way the latter tolerate nuclear weaponry, ignore pollution of the environment, and place self-interest before the general welfare. These differences in values have had an isolating effect on both groups. In addition, some young people feel alone because, not firmly a part of the overall culture, they also fail to accept their own special group.

Our economic system in the United States emphasizes the right to acquire wealth and worldly goods without much regard for the welfare of others. Cynically, people feel free to be aggressive, competitive, and even immoral. They take all that they can from society, returning to it only the little that they must. Any attempt to be their brother's keeper would tend to work against their success in business. In such an atmosphere it is difficult not to feel alone. This is particularly true for many ethnic minorities. Our economic system is especially unfavorable to them. And when their right to belong to the larger community is denied, they may feel more alone than ever.

While most people spend a major part of their lives at work, it is often difficult for them to relate to the total, completed product. Lawyers, doctors, dentists, therapists, accountants, or owners of businesses can relate more or less directly to the outcome of their work. But assembly-line workers can hardly feel great pride in their small contribution to the finished car, airplane, or washing machine. Unable to become absorbed in the mechanical motions that they perform and isolated from the total outcome, their work is not very meaningful to them. And this dissatisfaction with work cannot help but affect their view of their lives.

Physical attractiveness is especially important in our culture. People measure the worth of others by their appearance. They think less of men and women alike if they lack a flair for the latest fashions, or, especially insofar as the woman is concerned, if her measurements are not in line with what is considered attractive.

In such a superficial atmosphere it is not surprising that those who do not conform are thought to be dull, frowzy, and unattractive. Their physical makeup and grooming do not fit the picture that is now the style. Unless they are quite secure, they are likely to develop a rather poor picture of themselves. Once this happens, they feel isolated, with little hope of appealing to anyone worthwhile. There is a defensive element in their giving up hope, too—it keeps them from being disappointed and hurt. We are all familiar with the divorced couple who, hoping to form new relationships, first lose weight, get tans, select new wardrobes, and have their hair styled. They present their physical selves as if the packaging were more important than the contents. Men do this as frequently as women nowadays. They cultivate long hair and have it styled; they sport form-fitting clothes. Yet neither they nor their female counterparts may stop to consider the types of behavior that contributed to the divorce in the first place.

People whose attitude toward their physical selves is negative may lack poise and confidence, be reluctant to make a decision even about unimportant matters, or find it hard to stand up for their ideas. They may try to make up for their negative feelings by striving in the business world or in a profession, or by developing some outstanding skill. Their success will depend on whether they have the necessary intelligence, self-discipline, and motivation.

People who are physically disabled come in for more than their share of isolation. Their conditions exclude them from equal status with those who are able-bodied. Unfortunately, many of the latter tend to value appearances more than the total person. Physical deformity is an affront to them. Yet disabled people often mingle only with the able-bodied. Relationships with other disabled people would force them to face their disability, something they cannot do any better than those able-bodied people who reject them.

People who start to grow old also may become outcasts in our youth-oriented culture. Surrounded by others who dwell so heavily on physical externals, they lose status by growing old. As their powers wane, they become less interesting to others, who avoid them. They themselves find it more and more difficult to relate to those who have an outlook on life that is so different from their own. This is especially true if they have no close relationships. In addition, a deteriorating physical condition often brings a waning of the sexual drive that used to push them toward others. Also, it seems less worthwhile for them to take on long-range activities, particularly those that involve lengthy preparation. All this increases their feeling that they no longer are part of the stream of life. In time, approaching death further heightens their sense of aloneness.

In this chapter, various influences that contribute to the person's feelings of alienation have been described. Later chapters will offer suggestions on how to relieve these feelings.

Chapter 2

Anxiety

People who are frustrated in finding meaning in life are depressed and anxious. Anxiety is an uneasy state in which they are uncertain why they are troubled. They cannot relate their distress to anything in particular, but they cannot get rid of their feeling that something is wrong. That nothing awful ever happens to them is hardly reassuring.

Their anxiety sometimes produces physical symptoms such as headaches, dizziness, excessive perspiration, difficulty in sleeping, poor appetite, pounding heart, or painful muscular tension. They may be so tired that they feel completely drained, and this makes them feel even less capable of coping with life. Inevitably, they worry about their symptoms, which then adds to their anxiety.

A smoldering hostility is typical of the people who are alone. They try to keep it hidden as much as they can. They cannot express it openly because they are so dependent on the goodwill of those toward whom they are hostile. Convinced that they could never find anyone to replace those important people, they feel they had better not be antagonistic. Their hostility appears more in the form of silence, sarcasm, and depression. However, in certain women who cannot identify their anger and express it openly, it appears as tears. This will be discussed in some detail on page 16.

People who feel alone may have difficulty concentrating on whatever they are doing. They feel separated from it, as if they are not really participating in it. They do not value what they are doing *for its own sake*. They may be motivated to earn a living but not by the work itself. They may conform to what others expect of them so that they do many things without being at all interested in them. They may work toward a future goal that they hope will make them feel more secure or important, though the activity itself does not absorb them. It is difficult for them to engage in sex for its own sake rather than to prove themselves to be good lovers; to enjoy friends for themselves rather than to manipulate them for business purposes; to read in order to lose themselves in the content of a book rather than to be able to shine later in a discussion with friends.

They overevaluate themselves in some respects and underevaluate themselves in others. But their negative feelings predominate, and at times they seem unreal even to themselves and are convinced that they must appear so to others. If on occasion they do react favorably to someone, they are likely to be so desperate for companionship and understanding that they quickly form an intimate relationship. Most of the time it soon breaks down, and they retreat into their shells again.

They tend to have many inner conflicts. They wish consciously to behave in a certain way, but unconsciously they are driven to behave differently. They may need to accumulate a great deal of money in order to feel secure and important, but then they may have to spend money freely so that others will be impressed. They must remain married to feel that they are a success, yet it is difficult for them to adapt to the needs of their family members because they are so self-centered and withdrawn. Their families or friends reject them when they fail to adapt, and they react by withdrawing further.

Inevitably, they become even more self-centered. Tending to focus on how *they* feel and how *they* think, they are convinced that nobody in the world understands them. Then they feel sorry for themselves. Under these conditions, every little emotional setback seems large to them. They cannot get outside of themselves enough to put themselves in the shoes of the other person. The result is that they do not understand how others feel about things. The fewer the common understandings they share with others, the more isolated they feel, which makes it hard for them to really communicate with others.

Their life is dull. They feel that the years are wasting away. They go through the motions of living. In reaction to the emptiness of their life they dream and create fantasies about how to make it interesting and exciting. But their fantasies evaporate when it comes to taking steps to change them into reality.

Their aloneness is often the result of their having to put aside their needs for love and new experience so long that they are no longer aware of them. They think that their boredom is due to things outside themselves—their husbands, wives, jobs, hometowns, or whatever. They do not realize that boredom is a sign of depression, emptiness, and inability to make life meaningful.

In the hope of coming alive, people who are bored may seek sexual adventures. But these most likely will amount to little more than superficial physical contacts. An all too common picture is that of the man who, skilled in the social graces, participates in sex with a succession of women and never gets "involved." Afraid to commit himself, he remains impersonal in what should be the most personal of relationships. He is more interested in lovers as sexual objects than as people. He creates for himself the illusion of not being alone in the world through his "intimate" encounters. The illusion of a shared experience may lessen his immediate loneliness, but not his ever-present aloneness.

Some people pass their lives with others, but they do not experience satisfying relationships. They wonder why an intimate living situation, such as marriage or an affair, does not lessen their aloneness (as if empty gestures and physical contact could replace emotional closeness).

They may link themselves quickly but superficially to others they hardly know. Still, certain people cannot do even this. They can respond intensely only to a character or situation in a book or a movie. Though they become very emotional, they remain uninvolved. They can allow themselves intense feeling with a dramatic character because they are not risking anything in such a fantasy relationship. Sometimes the person cannot be emotionally close to others because unconsciously he or she desires someone else who is no longer available. Others substitute an attachment to their possessions, to animals, or to money for human closeness.

People who try to ignore the source of anxiety may become confused about their true feelings. By way of illustration, a woman consciously may want to be courted and get married. Marriage would satisfy her needs for love, sex, companionship, children, and a home. But unconsciously her drive may be blocked by guilt and fear. As a result, once the marriage date is set, she panics and feels that she must call off the wedding. She cannot understand her compulsion to do so because she is not aware of the extent to which her sexual problem influences her behavior.

People who cannot face their emotions may experience anxiety and depression. A man may be unable to concentrate, receive friends, or go to work. A woman is likely to find herself in tears as a result of her failure to recognize that she is angry. Wishing to be liked, she fears the displeasure or retaliation of others, and she fails to express her anger. As a result of not dealing with the issue that aroused her anger in the first place, she experiences her feelings as anxiety, fatigue, and depression. Carla and Bill are a good example.

Carla and Bill had been practically living together for about three months. Carla wanted Bill to declare his love and propose marriage. There were several reasons for this. She was not satisfied that it was proper for her to have sexual relations with him. Then, since she had serious doubts of her worth as a person, she needed to be reassured that he valued her highly. Having "given herself to Bill," she was deeply disappointed that he would not declare his undying love. She expected him to be so overwhelmed by his good fortune that he would insist on having her all to himself. But Bill, no more in love with her than she actually was with him, was not at all prepared to get married. He just was having an affair, and he wanted to keep it that way. Carla, denied the reassurance she needed so desperately, became very frustrated and angry. Bill could not understand the reason for her tears and depressed silences. He thought the two of them were very congenial—at least they never argued. But Carla had to terminate the relationship. The anger she tried to ignore took the form of such severe depression that she had come to fear she might break down altogether.

Carla's anxiety over expressing her anger caused her to ignore it, and that produced anxiety of its own. This invariably happens when the person distorts the truth of a situation. Sometimes a current situation cues the person back to an earlier one that had been put aside for many years. He becomes anxious out of all proportion to the threat contained in the current situation because he experiences feelings raised by the earlier situation, too. Or, a given need may be in conflict with another need of which the person is not aware. She finds herself torn in two directions. She may unconsciously fear giving in to a desire to smoke, drink, eat, use drugs, or have sexual relations. Yet she has a need to conform to her group, which expects her to do these things. A person may become anxious at the thought of performing a dishonest or selfish act. Unconsciously he wants to perform it, or he has already done so in another situation that he has buried in his mind.

Because all of these reactions take place on an unconscious level, people have little insight to the cause of their anxiety. They know only that at times they perspire freely when there seems to be no reason to do so. They feel muscles tensing so much that they are painful. They have knots in their stomach or feel generally upset. Through it all they sense a vague threat from a source that they cannot identify.

The more insight people can gain to the sources of their anxiety, the better they will deal with it. But when they cannot tell what these sources are, they may do one of two things. They merely may endure the anxiety or they may ease it by developing symptoms. If a young man feels clumsy and out of place at a college dance, he may stand on the sidelines and eat his heart out, or he may discuss philosophy learnedly with a male friend. All his talk—the symptom—is simply his way of pretending that he does not want to hold a girl in his arms and dance with her. Actually, he is too self-conscious to do so. Or, if a coed is afraid to face an exam for which she has not studied, she may play the game with herself of feeling too ill to take it. The physical symptoms that she talks herself into protect her against failure on the exam. This reinforces her repeated use of such symptoms. But the symptoms themselves breed new anxieties by limiting her behavior. She fails to take the examination. In the long run, her failure to place herself in a situation that, though stressful, is essential to getting her degree arouses even greater anxiety in her than if she had faced up to the examination and done poorly.

There are many other situations in which people escape natural anxiety only to find that in the long run they are in for much greater neurotic anxiety. They may unconsciously avoid a person they regard as equal or superior to themselves. They feel unsure of themselves with such a person. Or they may be drawn to a person precisely because he or she appears to be woefully inadequate. They are not afraid of being rejected because they feel adequate with such people. But soon they are disturbed by the other person's inferiority because it is deflating to them to be linked with an inferior, immature, or dull person. This gives them a poor picture of themselves.

Sometimes people unconsciously transfer attitudes from prior situations to current ones. In doing so, they experience the anxiety of the prior situations even though there is no valid basis for doing so. Instead of being natural, as it may have been in the prior situations, their anxiety is now neurotic because it is not inherent in the current situation. Mel and Jane are good examples of this.

Mel, forty, has been married for ten years to Jane, thirty. Their relationship is superficial and lacks warmth. Their sexual interaction is poor. They would probably divorce were it not for their two children. As it is, they each have fantasies of parting and finding more exciting partners and they each deal differently with the frustration of their needs for understanding, warmth, love, and emotional security.

Mel, who cannot fall asleep, tries to escape his painful aloneness—at about one or two in the morning—by having a few stiff drinks and then gorging himself on whatever happens to be in the refrigerator. Sometimes even this is not enough, and he masturbates to rid himself of his ever-present sexual desire. He would like to express it toward Jane, but he feels too hostile to do so. While he makes his life bearable for the moment by sleeping and forgetting, he worries about his growing dependence on alcohol (he drinks at dinner, too). He knows that he cannot do without it.

For her part, Jane escapes into a round of telephone calls, shopping for clothes, browsing for antiques, beauty shop visits (she is very concerned about growing old), and fantasies of doing interesting and exciting things. This is how she tries to dismiss her feelings of insecurity.

Many of their difficulties stem from Jane's conviction that she can never really depend on Mel, that he will only let her down. Though Mel is an extremely responsible person, she responds to him as she did to other figures in her life who did let her down badly. In doing so, she sacrifices some of the *reality* of Mel. Her anticipation that he, like the others, would surely let her down has prevented her from ever being close to him.

When people make a choice, they often do whatever will ease their anxiety then and there. As a result, they may fail to move on to more satisfying levels of behavior. I have described this (in *Effective Personality: a Humanistic Approach*, Wadsworth Publishing Co., Monterey, California, 1972) as follows:

> It is a delicate task for the person to maintain an identity firm enough to allow him to retain the integrity of his personality, yet flexible enough for him to undergo transformation. He is impelled to grow and develop to avoid becoming stagnant. Yet, apprehensive of what growth may entail, he is constrained to remain on any plateau of security he has already achieved. *Thus, he puts off the anxiety that is always implicit in new experience until such time as he can come to terms with it.* As he encounters successive crossroads of choice, his life experience and conditioning (and, I might add here, his ability to tolerate natural anxiety) will influence his capacity to mature.

Frustration and the behavior to which it gives rise are closely related to anxiety. But it must not be assumed that a frustrating situation always arouses anxiety. The person may adapt and forestall the anxiety he or she might have felt. This capacity depends on the flexibility with which an individual shifts from one approach to another, as well as the development of essential emotional, physical, or mental skills.

While there are many personal sources of frustration and anxiety, the environment is a frequent source, too. There is a ferment in society today that can frustrate even the most stable and mature person. Economic stress, social change, the role dislocation for both men and women due to the women's liberation movement, conflict over civil rights, the hostility among ethnic groups—all result in a great deal of frustration. And there is always the cynical impersonality of so many organizations within which people work.

The numerous standards to which one feels compelled to conform are frustrating too. A young man, not wishing to appear cheap, may spend more than he can afford on a date. He becomes anxious not only about what he spends, but about maintaining that level of spending. Still, he is eager to make a good impression. For her part, a young woman may feel compelled to spend money on clothes that she cannot afford. But she may feel that to make an equally good impression her grooming must be in the latest fashion.

The person's need to like himself causes, among other types of anxiety, one that may be called *false guilt*. This appears when a person behaves in some way that is different from how he thinks he should. Such guilt is a way of paying lip service to behavior that he is *not* prepared to carry out. It is as if he were to say, "I really am a very decent sort of person, and when I do something like this it is very upsetting to me." His guilty reaction is a game that he plays to think well of himself *while continuing his exploitative behavior*. He becomes anxious about his picture of himself and invents the guilt because he is aware on some level that he does not intend to change. If he does change his behavior, then his guilt is no longer false.

Henry, forty-four, had quite a way with women. He was quick to get into intimate relationships with them, and somehow conveyed that he was looking for a wife. He had many material things to offer and was rather handsome. But no sooner did a woman give any sign of being interested in him as a husband than he started withdrawing from her. He was a skilled "sharpshooter" and could easily find something wrong with any woman. He used this to justify loss of the interest that he never really had. Of course, the woman, who had felt quite encouraged by him and had allowed herself to make general plans for the future, was baffled and hurt by his seeming turnabout. And she was likely to tell him so sooner or later. Then Henry became contrite, upset, and felt *so* guilty that he had led her on and obtained her favors! But he refused to admit that on some level he had known all along that he was not seriously interested in her. Yet, no sooner had he ended one relationship than he involved himself in a new one, using the very same approach. His guilt was as false as his intentions to marry the girl.

Since it may be painful for people to be anxious, they

try to avoid certain situations. Otherwise, they have to endure the anxiety. But the more aware of their motives they are, the more difficult it is for them to block out the anxiety by playing deceptive games with themselves. To the extent that they do play games, they fail to deal directly and realistically with the situation arousing the anxiety. *Instead, they perform other behavior.* This is their way of trying to relieve the anxiety. But when they substitute other behavior, they distort the true emotion. If they are afraid to express their anger, for example, they may initiate sexual relations instead, hoping to convince their partner that they have feelings of love. This relieves the anxiety that they would feel were they to express their anger. In time, this unconscious game becomes their customary way of dealing with their anger.

Their substitutive behavior allows them to escape, though unaware that they are doing so, from a situation that they do not have the resources to face. For example, any time that Caroline sensed the merest beginnings of a sexual overture, she became very talkative and intellectual with a man. Her barrage of words enabled her to keep her sexual needs repressed.

While substitutive behavior enables the person to retain a favorable picture of him or herself it does not lead to the satisfaction of repressed needs.

Sometimes there is no way the person can do anything directly about a frustrating situation. For example, vain and self-centered, though feeling basically unimportant, she may wish to become a well-known actress. But if she simply does not have the particular abilities that this requires, she may substitute another activity that she *is* able to carry out. She may become an English teacher and still hold forth before an admiring and captive audience. In this way she gains some indirect satisfaction of her need. This points to the realistic quality of her attitude toward life, for she recognizes what she can and cannot do. Her substitutive behavior enables her to tolerate the frustration.

A person may also employ fantasy to great advantage.

He pictures what he hopes to do, feeling his way into it. But his fantasy is constructive only if he follows it up with concrete steps aimed at making it a reality. If he substitutes fantasy for actual behavior, it leaves him open to anxiety stemming from unfulfilled need. Then he pays a heavy price for his escape from the reality of the situation.

Chapter 3

The Need for Meaning

Human beings have a great need to understand the environment in which they exist. This has been true for their social, personal, and physical environments. Without such understanding they can hardly find meaning in life. Ancient man had this problem, too. Though he did not understand many things in his environment—illness, natural catastrophes, the seasons, and emotional disorder—he was forced to come to grips with them. He did this through superstition and a belief in spirits and magic. This was his way of not allowing his fear of the unknown to destroy his sense of orderly, meaningful living.

Ancient man was convinced that if he wished for something sincerely enough, he could bring it about. While this gave him no more than a fantasized sense of power, he could at least face a world that was mysterious and threatening in many ways. Events that otherwise would have seemed strange and without purpose became meaningful to him. But, of course, while what a person believes may be real to him it may not be at all helpful in coping with a situation.

If ancient man was superstitious, modern man, as recently as 200 to 400 years ago, had not discarded his belief in the occult. We have only to think of the witches of Salem to realize this. And certainly contemporary man is capable of magical and superstitious thinking. For example, a young college graduate fantasizes his father dead each time the latter flies east on business. He is aware that lurking just beneath his fantasy is the wish that his father be eliminated from his life. One day the father's plane crashes and the father dies. Now the son is obsessed with guilt. He is convinced that he murdered his father by wishing him dead. Many recent films abundantly illustrate this belief in the power of magic and superstition.

Today people face life on a level of threat that exceeds anything ancient or modern man ever had to face before—the threat of nuclear war. While only a few people are openly concerned about it, no one can ignore it altogether. Most people busy themselves with the everyday affairs of life—working, loving, playing, dreaming, creating. May it not be magical thinking that enables them to pursue their daily lives in the face of such potential destruction? Sometimes contemporary man, like ancient and modern man, believes whatever he needs to believe in order to feel secure and retain a sense of meaning in life.

Many people believe in a personal deity, a kind, all-powerful, all-knowing being such as the Christian God. Yet it is impossible for others to live in the world, *aware*, and continue to believe because God, if one exists, seems so indifferent to their pain. They cannot blind themselves to the accidents, catastrophes, and evils that surround them. Four little children and their mother are burned to death in a fire; terrorist hijackers kill forty innocent passengers in an attempt to save the lives of two members of their group, both murderers; a car driven by a drunk kills a person in another car; in broad daylight, fifteen teenage boys beat an old man to death in the center of a busy metropolis, and no one goes to his aid; a woman suffers the humiliation of being raped by an unknown assailant, who then murders her; nations devise flame throwers, nerve gases, and hydrogen bombs of hideously destructive power with which they maim and kill millions; even men of God, some of whom would give up life rather than deviate from their faith, may be dedicated to the most sordid enterprises in which they kill others over religion itself, making a cruel hoax of it. It is not easy for some people to believe in a God of tenderness and mercy when they are surrounded by so much pain and viciousness. And, unable to believe, they cannot ease their aloneness. But others, through faith, feel secure in the face of potential accident, illness, or natural catastrophe, though the environment may not justify their feeling.

The earth is a very small part of an endless universe. In all this great universe have we humans been singled out as chosen by God, indeed, created in his image, as many people believe? Do they believe this because otherwise they would feel reduced to nothingness and would lose being? Do they embrace this reassuring belief because they feel helpless and alone if they do not?

Many people reject the idea of a personal God. They believe in an impersonal force or law that regulates the universe and makes it orderly and safe. But their sense of being alone in a vast, unfeeling universe may be intense. The order of the universe is not always favorable to their welfare, or even to their survival. Belief in a cosmic order is of dubious value in protecting them from the accident, pain, and trauma that are so widespread.

It is not surprising, then, that life may appear to be utterly absurd and without purpose or meaning. There seems to be no ultimate source of caring. Nor is there an ultimate source of justice, for the most undeserved tragedies happen to fine and worthy people.

Certain Eastern sages find through their own beliefs the same reassurance that Western religions offer us. For them, the person is not separate and, therefore, not alone. They conceive of us all as being a part of life and nature. To them apartness is an illusion. Believing destroys the illusion.

Now, it is certain that we are all a part of nature and feel a kinship not only with many people but also with animals. But it is also certain that we can feel very alone in the world.

People may puff themselves up with mighty plans, but life often reduces these to piffling unimportance. If they try to sustain themselves on a belief in fate, they may not escape the absurdity of life. Perhaps this is what Shakespeare had in mind when he had Macbeth say (Act V, Scene V):

> Tomorrow, and tomorrow, and tomorrow
> Creeps in this petty pace from day to day
> To the last syllable of recorded time.
> And all our yesterdays have lighted fools
> The way to dusty death. Out, out, brief candle!
> Life's but a walking shadow, a poor player
> That struts and frets his hour upon the stage
> And then is heard no more. It is a tale
> Told by an idiot, full of sound and fury,
> Signifying nothing.

Science has shed considerable light on the physical laws that govern the earth. It has penetrated the biological nature of man, and it has gained insight to a great deal of his psychological functions. At the same time, life has come to be understood in a setting of social, political, economic, and technological factors. Our beliefs and attitudes are influenced by objective data so much more today than they ever were in the times of ancient or modern man. This enables the contemporary person to experience meaning that is more consistent with reality and does not depend on superstition.

Fortunately, although we are subject to the despair arising from natural and man-made catastrophes, we also can experience joy, love, achievement, mutual understanding, creativity, compassion, generosity, intellectual activity, and friendship. The important difference, so far as we are concerned, is that so much of our despair springs from the nature of life and the environment, while joy and love and friendship are *created* by humans through the values and goals to which they adhere and the relationships in which they become involved.

Most of the time people have no way of knowing that what appears to be reality is only subjectively real. What is reality to them is not necessarily in the situation alone but also in their perception of it. It would be easier to grasp a fixed reality if it were external to them. But because their reality is subjective, arising from their values, goals, and personality, they can seldom know some final objective reality. As a result, they may build their life around relationships that are unreliable or inappropriate. A woman may feel secure with her lover, though actually he may be very involved with someone else. She has chosen to ignore various bits of evidence that might tell her what she is not prepared to face. While what the person believes to be fact makes up what reality is to him, all realities are not equally factual or fulfilling.

People in different societies have different concepts of what is meaningful to them. And within any society what is meaningful varies from one subculture to another. Actually, it varies from person to person, as we have seen. There are many realities, and all are true for those who adhere to them. The person may accept as absolutely true the biblical version of the creation of the universe and of man's exalted place within it. There is a reality of the middle class and that of the common man, the conscious and the unconscious, the objective and the subjective, the psychotic and the normal, the secular and the religious, and many others. Not only do people create their own reality in response to their need to find meaning in life, but, as they develop personally and socially, their reality keeps changing.

While it is true that humans do not feel so alone when they create meaning, if what is meaningful to them is quite different from what is meaningful to the figures close to them—wife, husband, children, business associates, relatives, friends—it will not offset their aloneness very well. It is largely through *shared* meaning that they can insulate themselves from their aloneness. Marriage remains a vital institution because within it people can share their values and ways of doing things. The sense of close relationship that arises when two people share meaning combats their aloneness. Andras Angyal, an astute observer, has said of close relationship (in his *Neurosis and Treatment*): "We are nothing within ourselves, nonexistent. To be is to mean something to someone else. This existence we cannot directly create for ourselves; it can only be given to us by another."

The meaning that people create is not always sustained. Their close relationships may be dissolved, their achievements may crumble, their love and joy may disappear, and their friendships may end. Their compassion and caring may run dry, and their understanding and generosity may end in a war's maiming and killing. Yet they can recapture these lost qualities in new situations.

When the meaning that humans create turns out to be fleeting, life becomes meaningless to them. They may give up hope of ever finding anything that will make it seem worthwhile. Exhausted by their unfulfilled need for meaning, they resign themselves to depression and loss of hope. Betty is a good example.

At twenty-eight Betty had not yet made anything of her life. Since graduating from high school, she had gone through a number of jobs, never seeming to find the one that suited her. She had been fired from most of them for tardiness, absenteeism, and an inability to concentrate and get her work done on time. She was listless, dull, bored, and always tired. She derived very little meaning from her job.

Betty was just as disorganized, tired, and "down" in her personal life. She had many physical complaints, though a checkup showed her to be in average health. She explained her failure to keep up her little apartment as due to her fatigue and illness. She had the same explanation for her failure to develop hobbies and interests. Oddly though, if there was something she really wanted to do (like visit a girl friend at nine in the evening) she seemed to have all kinds of energy.

Betty seldom dated, but when she did she was a sexual pushover. She was not a passionate woman; it was simply that she hoped to hold a man's interest in this way. She would cling to him just as long as he would let her, which was usually no more than a week or two. She discussed her physical symptoms, got him to fix things around her apartment, and controlled their activities through her fatigue and other complaints. Of course, this drove the man away.

Deprived of relationship, regarding herself as ill, frustrated at work, and beset by money problems, there was little that Betty could fall back on to sustain herself. She was very discouraged about ever making a life for herself, either in the home or in the business world. Her life had so little meaning that she felt her aloneness keenly and had begun to think about suicide.

When people are deprived of meaning through illness, accident, death of a loved one, or loss of status or material things, if they can accept these events as part of life they will then create new meaning by replacing what has been lost as best they can. The more meaning they create, the less likely they are to resign themselves to death. They have more to lose. Yet they can accept death better when it comes, knowing that they have had a full and rewarding life.

Human beings create meaning when they conform to society and accept the importance of doing things in certain ways. However, this is true only if they enjoy a sense of belonging as a result of their conformity. It is not true if they are rebellious inwardly while they conform outwardly.

If it is meaningful to acquire wealth and gain status, it is because we have decided that it is important to do so. In other societies these goals may be regarded as wasted time and energy. From a variety of values and goals, people choose those that create meaning *for them.* Their participation in our social institutions helps them feel that they are not alone.

Many people become restless and dissatisfied when

their life is superficial. They have a need to find deeper meaning. Despite our society's emphasis on achievement, money, and status, unless they can combine their self-interest with the welfare of others they may feel that their life is of no particular importance. Thus, Sarah was determined to expand her life.

Sarah is fifty-three, single, and has been self-supporting all her adult life. With some sacrifice she has managed to put aside $8,000 out of her salary as a secretary. This money is not for her retirement. Sarah becomes animated when she explains that in another two years she will retire as a secretary and start a whole new life operating her own preschool nursery. She is completing a course of study in the evening that will equip her for this on a professional basis. "I do have to support myself," she says, "but there has to be some time in my life when I can take a real part in the lives of others and do some good."

If our impersonal society has not made it easy for Sarah to combine self-interest with a concern for others, her need for meaning causes her to do so.

When humans cannot picture an acceptable future, their life seems empty and meaningless. Hope is like a bridge that extends from their empty life to a future that will be fulfilling. This bridge of hope helps them look beyond the painful present. Their behavior reveals whether they have lost hope. The former tuberculosis patient, for example, who lives in the smog-ridden climate of Los Angeles, but persists in smoking three to four packs of cigarettes a day, is destroying herself. The same may be said of the alcoholic young woman, who, feeling at odds with life, is developing cirrhosis of the liver but will not stop drinking. Many people partially give up life as they lose hope of ever making their lives meaningful. Complete loss of hope may lead to suicide.

It is the inborn drive of human beings to expand their life that pushes them to develop themselves. In doing so they create sufficient meaning to block out aloneness and anxiety. Under such conditions they are fully expressive in their personal relationships. While absorbed in long-range goals, they also live in the here and now and satisfy more immediate goals. They are their own people and can stand alone against others when necessary. They have a satisfying picture of themselves. They shape the direction of their lives to an important degree. As a result they seldom feel themselves to be at the mercy of fate or chance. They are usually involved both within the home and outside it. They have a strong sense of belonging and feel themselves to be part of the important trends of the day. Their involvement makes them feel needed and gives them purpose and direction in life. This is why they are men and women of the future more than of the present or past. They are filled with hope for a better self and a better world. In one way or another, they contribute to those about them. They find life rewarding because they create so much meaning.

It is more difficult to create meaning today than it was about seventy-five years ago. At that time parents and their children spent much more time together than they do today. A large part of the population lived on small farms, and there were many more small shops and independent artisans. Closer ties within the family and between the generations were possible. Parents served as models to be imitated by their children to a much greater extent. The capacity to earn a living was a primary value. The work that parents and children did together was essential to the maintenance of the home, and this gave the young person *a sense of being needed, of making a difference.* In turn, his or her relationships were intensified and their feelings of worth and importance were increased. Their life was filled with direction and purpose. As opposed to the self-centeredness of today's small family, they were much more involved in satisfying the needs of others in the larger family that was common at the turn of the century.

Today most of our population lives in the cities; at the turn of the century about seventy percent lived on farms—now only about seven percent do. The independent workman or farmer has for the most part been absorbed into large-scale industry. Not too much work that is essential and saves money is performed in the home. These activities are carried on outside the home—educational studies by the university, training in the arts by specialized schools, and the development of occupational skills by business and educational organizations. These institutions can be so impersonal and large—the immense campus, the huge corporation, the highly structured governmental department—that people may hardly feel they belong and so many suffer a loss of meaning. Meanwhile, the many services that used to be so time-consuming in the home—laundering, baking, needlecraft—no longer are. These used to foster interaction within the family and promote closer ties, making life more meaningful.

It is in the home that children first learn to create meaning. While they may expand this capacity in later life, it is always influenced by what they learned while growing up.

Part Two

How We Create Meaning

The person can insulate himself from the absurdity and aloneness of life and make it meaningful. The most important ways in which this can be done are described in pairs of chapters in this section. The second chapter illustrates the concepts of the first.

Chapter 4

Close Relationship

As a result of their prolonged dependence on their parents, children remain in intimate relationship with them for a long time. Their idea of love is shaped not only by the *sustained quality of their relationship* but also by their more or less *exclusive possession of the interest and attention of their parents.*

Love is fleeting and elusive. As we grasp it, we find to our dismay that we cannot give ourselves to the one we love—sweetheart, husband, wife, child, brother, friend—as fully and continuously as we desire. We are too wrapped up in our own selves to embrace the other fully and surrender ourselves to love. We are too centered in ourselves. It is our nature to remain separate despite our need to remove the wall between ourselves and others. This limitation on our love gives rise to aloneness even as we mingle ourselves with a partner.

At first a person in a relationship (married or otherwise) pictures the partner only partially, ignoring what he or she does not want to see. He creates an idealized picture of her, as does she of him. When they come face to face with the total reality of each other, their fantasy is destroyed. So they love as best they can but never as fully as they would like.

The love that they enjoyed at home influences the quality of their adult love. If the childhood emphasis on being loved and taken care of was not gradually shifted to loving actively by satisfying the needs of others, they will run into trouble in their adult relationships. At first the mutual satisfaction of basic needs may embrace no more than sexual attraction and certain interests that they have in common. But unless they become more deeply involved, their relationship is likely soon to run its course.

The ending of their relationship may be precipitated by one partner pursuing various members of the opposite sex. But this often would be intolerable to the other partner. So to maintain their relationship each agrees to thwart the physical and psychological side of his or her nature to cater to the trained side. But as they make this uneasy truce with their nature, their love may become an embattled thing.

However, this conflict in the person's love may be undergoing change at the present time. In response to social, economic, and liberating influences, for example, more and more mothers are following their own interests shortly after giving birth. This results in the child being less dependent on his mother's attention and love. He learns to seek these from a variety of sources. As an adult, he may then be able to participate *in a number of personal relationships without feeling guilty*. And this does not imply that as an adult such a child will become promiscuous—but rather that he or she will not adhere as strongly to fidelity as a value that if violated is likely to disrupt a marriage. And he or she may be capable of accepting this in a partner, too. Then this conflict in love may not be so severe or may disappear altogether in some cases.

The core of the person's feeling of being loved is *feeling understood*. He or she does not feel so alone when understood. A partner can share in the deeper side of the other's life only to the extent that she or he understands the other. Considerable time and effort are required to do this, as is open communication. The person who can offer these qualities becomes special to a partner, who then is less inclined to turn to someone else.

In open communication people reveal themselves without fear, letting their partner into their thoughts and feelings. Each is put into the other's shoes and sees things from the other's point of view. They arrive at common meanings with each other by sharing thoughts and feelings. They listen sensitively both to the surface words and to the underlying meanings. This conveys the importance they attach to the other. Even facial expressions and small movements reveal the depth of their attention. They must have a deep interest and concern in each other if they are to put forth the continuous effort required for mutual understanding.

When trying to communicate, two people may disagree not only on what has occurred but also why it has occurred. This tends to happen when they are insecure, for then they need to be right—even when they are wrong. People who are secure can change their ideas, but those who are insecure cling rigidly to their own point of view. Their unconscious attitudes, prejudices, fears, and values distort their reaction to the issue and their partner.

A person may not accept the differences between himself and his partner. He then tries to persuade her to see things his way. But this only calls forth her resistance. If he really wants to understand her he needs to talk in a *nonpersuasive* way instead of trying to influence how she will think. This is much more effective in bridging the gaps between them. Thus, when they differ, each states the situation from his or her perspective. Refusing to defend or "sell" a point of view, each merely *describes* it. This gives them both a chance to understand exactly what the other feels and expects.

However, nonpersuasive communication is persuasive in an indirect way. This is because the partners in a relationship want to bridge the gaps between them. Each hopes to fulfill the other's needs and expectations. Unless this happens they will hardly contribute to the meaningfulness of their life, to whatever extent they may share it. So there is a subtle pressure to satisfy each other once their true feelings are known.

A couple must accept each other if they are to communicate well. To accept is for each to allow the other to be the way he or she is without trying to effect a change in personality. And at no time does the person think less of a partner for being different. One who is not acceptant sees the other's behavior as a personal affront. He or she cannot be involved with a partner and remain detached from his or her behavior. They become isolated from each other because they are different in some way deemed especially important. Failure of one partner to accept the other prevents the rejected one from revealing his or her true feelings. But if they accept each other, then when they see faults in each other, they do not allow these to influence negatively the *entire* image they have of each other. Of course, acceptance implies approval of the other in many respects, too.

When two people react differently to an issue, this does not necessarily mean that one is right and the other wrong. Nor does it mean that one of them is superior, the other inferior. It may mean only that they are different. Often it takes a great deal of time and discussion just to pinpoint differences. But if they hope to be acceptant, each of them must not only do this but must also understand the motives behind the other's behavior and what that behavior means to his or her self-image.

The person's capacity to become involved with someone of the opposite sex is usually essential to well-being and development; yet, all too often, the urge to reach out for love is blocked by fear. Some people are so afraid of being hurt that, isolating themselves from warmth and love, they hurt very much. Because they have a poor picture of themselves, they may be convinced that they will be rejected.

They may be so overdependent on a rather distant relationship that they cling to it. Yet they do so in a cold, withdrawn way. They need a great deal of proof before they feel that their partner cares for them, but they seldom get it. Then they feel uncared for, with no one in the whole world to lean on. They become quite depressed as they fail to create meaning in life through close relationships.

Almost all experience—a walk in the park, a good movie, a delicious meal, playing with a charming and happy child—becomes more meaningful when it is shared. It is not so much what things two people do together as that they do them *together*. No matter how much meaning people create by themselves, they seem to require a close relationship to become whole. In a physical sense they can exist alone and be complete. But emotionally they are not complete persons by themselves. The closer the relationship with a partner is, the more each helps the other to create meaning.

Certain people remain single not because they cannot relate closely but because they are critical of marriage. They see it as a type of relationship that is personally frustrating because it restricts their freedom. Yet they may be quite capable of allowing others to become very important in their lives.

But other single people resist relationships because they fear them. As a result they ordinarily are more aware of how alone they are than someone who is involved in a serious relationship. Their efforts to create meaning through a relationship are likely to take the form of a series of superficial and brief affairs. These brief relationships often do not create as much meaning as one that is more lasting. Feeling needed is essential to the creation of meaning, and the person is more likely to feel that his or her partner depends heavily on him or her when they are involved for a long time.

Perhaps one of the major influences that makes for the transient affair is romantic love. This type of love is centered on one person's idealization of another and today emphasizes sexual relations. But after they have come through a succession of romantic affairs, they may feel very isolated. These do not prepare them for close and lasting relationships. When they lose hope of ever finding such a relationship, they can hardly endure the aloneness that engulfs them. They are frustrated in a basic need—to share in each other.

Our movies, songs, and novels keep the romantic concept of choosing a partner for love alone very much alive. Modern technology has done much to destroy the image of the woman as a household drudge. Her ability to support herself is also favorable to a choice based on love. The declining authority of parents within the home frees the young person to choose a partner for love and with little regard for the values that may be crucial to the success of a marriage.

Intense feeling dominates romantic love. There is little emphasis on the capacity to satisfy a broad range of basic needs, so romantic love cannot sustain itself. Also, daily and intimate exposure of two people to one another shatters the unrealistic, idealized way they see each other. But the person tends to select a partner on a romantic basis for a relationship that rapidly loses its romantic atmosphere. If one sees anything negative in a partner that would discourage marriage, he or she may ignore it if possible. This is because each of them may desire sexual relations urgently. Also, they may need to prove that they are attractive enough to obtain a spouse whom they can possess exclusively.

Many a young woman, feeling desperately alone and determined not to spend one more evening with her television set, accepts a date from which she returns home more depressed than ever. This does not ease her aloneness at all. It is not easy for her to accept that the best she can do is to have a date with someone she finds undesirable. She ventures forth only because she needs and hopes to find someone with whom she can experience mutual love, care, understanding, sympathy, and companionship. When her life is unshared it hardly seems worthwhile. A close relationship would bring her values and goals into play, intensifying her sense of meaningful living.

Though the person meets much of the need to relate to others through membership in the family, the approval and acceptance of friends also contribute to feelings of adequacy. He or she enjoys feelings of warmth, respect, and companionship with them. They may be organized loosely in a group devoted to any purpose whatsoever, just so long as the person is really interested in it. But merely being a member of the group will not provide a sense of belonging or create meaning. If a person exploits the group for personal ends, he or she cannot feel a sense of belonging. For example, a man may be an insurance salesman and may join the group in the hope of making business contacts. But his intentions will soon be discovered by the others, and in one way or another they will manage to exclude him.

Until a person becomes a valued part of some circle of friends, he tends to feel alone to some extent. Such isolation may be due to a fear of being hurt. But in trying to feel better about one's self, one may decide defensively that most people are too ordinary to mingle with. Some people insist that they would rather be alone than fritter away time on superficial people. They maintain that their values are so different (superior) from those of the average person that it's not worth the effort to try to get along with them when life is so short. Underneath, however, they are depressed as a result of a vague awareness of not expressing the inborn need to belong.

Unless the person conforms to the conventional patterns of sexual behavior, he will have difficulty feeling that he belongs. Even when he relates to both sexes, he tends to feel that he is an outsider. In that case, he seldom relates closely to either sex, so that he has no clear-cut picture of his sexual identity. This colors all feelings about himself. Failing to feel that he belongs to society as a whole, he suffers from his aloneness.

Chapter 5

Fidelity With Zest

The most common setting for close relationships is marriage. A partner who stands at the person's side eases aloneness. One may tend to feel insecure in the face of social change—sexual attitudes that violate traditional values, women's adoption of new roles as they free themselves from a subordinate position within the home, urbanization that makes for anonymity and isolation, increased mobility in response to job demands, and the unrest among minority groups. So, one looks to a partner as an emotional mainstay.

But despite change, marriage *as an institution* is stronger today than ever before. That is, despite the increase in divorce, the net number per thousand who are married is greater. Its strength is due in part to the very changes that have taken place. Husbands and wives are more dependent on one another because of the impersonal atmosphere of our large cities. This is particularly true when they move about the country to take advantage of better job opportunities. Today a large number of parents support their children when the children marry young. That divorces are easier to obtain has strengthened the institution of marriage by encouraging people who are reluctant to commit themselves to take a chance.

Marriage is also stronger as an intimate setting for love and sexuality. Nowadays there is more equality of the partners. Communication between them is more open. And they are much more free sexually. But it must be admitted that, though they are more open and free, all too often love and sex do not exactly flourish within the restraints of marriage. Yet it is to satisfy these very needs that two people get married in the first place.

Despite the limitations of marriage, however, most people want to get married. Some even do so a number of times. Those who do not marry tend to feel that one of life's most significant experiences has eluded them. Certainly the emotional interaction among the members of the family makes marriage a lifestyle that can be meaningful. The roles played within it and its lasting nature also make it meaningful.

Perhaps by bearing children women create more meaning than men. They feel creative as the child develops within them. However, many men come to regard their children as their most worthwhile achievement. They may claim their children's accomplishments as if they were directly responsible for them. But once their offspring grow older or when they leave home to make lives of their own, many parents may feel their aloneness more keenly. They are no longer at the center of much of their children's lives, though they may wish the children would continue to be the center of theirs.

As people play the roles of wife, husband, mother, father, homemaker, or provider, they recreate the family scene to which they became so strongly conditioned during their prolonged dependence as children on their family. Marriage gives continuity to their lives. This is one of the major reasons that marriage has endured as a lifestyle. The creation of this situation is one of their strongest bulwarks against aloneness. They cling to marriage even when they are not too happy with their partner. They tolerate being alone poorly. Though they may not be aware of it, the pain of a divorce is often due more to giving up the *structure* of a husband or wife, children, home, and circle of friends than to losing their partner.

Though their difficulties appear in the marital interaction, the origin lies in the faulty patterns of personality they have been developing since early childhood.

They may hardly be prepared for marriage. They could realize its potentials for happiness better if their capacity to satisfy another's needs were encouraged within the parental home; if prolonged adolescence were accompanied by greater responsibility; if sexual guilt were lightened; if the educational system, from grade school through college, took more responsibility for instruction about sex, dating, marriage, child rearing, and the psychology of interpersonal interaction; if movies and television abandoned their romantic presentation of life more than they already have, and, finally, if they were trained to cope with shifting concepts of their roles, for these are in transition today more than ever before.

People bring all their personal illusions to marriage. When these lead to failure, they may find fault with marriage rather than with themselves. Marriage tests their faulty patterns of personality, bringing them to light under the pressure of living day after day with the same partner, the same responsibilities, and the same restrictions on behavior. It is no small matter to function maturely within marriage, to adapt one's behavior to the needs of the family without sacrificing one's own personality.

Each partner wants certain things. But if he or she has to ask for them or if they are given reluctantly, they fail to be satisfying. Each partner wants complete trust and loyalty; each wants sexual responsiveness; each wants sustained interest, attention, and affection; each wants to be admired and esteemed; each wants to be understood intimately; each wants respect, as well as tolerance for shortcomings; each wants the other to focus on the good points of the marriage and to communicate these positive feelings. Each wants the satisfaction of knowing that he or she has gratified the other's deepest needs.

In addition to being sexually responsive, those who are married are called on to remain emotionally involved with their partner. They must sustain this dual interest for a great many years. And they must sustain it exclusively with their partner. *This is the primary challenge of marriage.* Despite an urge to know others, a person is expected to set up a lasting love situation with just one person.

Though children are loving and affectionate with their parents, they are not permitted to be sexual with them. This denial of sexual attraction lasts for the fifteen to eighteen years that they are growing to adulthood. They are trained thoroughly to restrain sexual response toward those they love. When it is essential to combine it with love later on in marriage, they may have great difficulty doing so. This was the case with Gordon.

Gordon had every intention of remaining faithful to Ardis when he took the marriage vow. But what he had not anticipated was that he would no longer be able to react sexually to her once they had their children and she made the transition from sweetheart to mother. Unaware of what motivated him, he thought his sexual frustration was due to the way Ardis had let herself go. How was he to know that Margaret, a girl he had known intimately before she married, would become divorced, would call him at work and want to pick up where they had left off some years before? Or that Margaret, who now worked in an office, would always be dressed to kill and look just—well, you know.

Clearly, no one could have expected Gordon to foresee all this. No, it was hardly his fault that he and Margaret had become intimate again, the way they felt about each other, and the way Ardis treated him, paying more attention to the children than to him. His arguments were very convincing—to himself. He had not arranged for an interview with a psychologist because of his affair with Margaret. No, no! It was that Ardis was always nagging and picking at him, so that they argued constantly. "Doctor, that woman won't leave me alone for a single minute when I'm home! She bitches at me all the time! I tell you, I can hardly stand it! God, if I couldn't get out of the house once in a while and have a little fun I'd go crazy!"

Whenever Gordon felt he simply had to get out of the house to see Margaret, he would start an argument with Ardis. It was always over something he knew she could not help. One of his favorites was to criticize her (already overweight as she was) for eating too much, especially sweets. Yet he never did a thing to help her with her problem. He insisted she keep ice cream, cake, nuts, and chocolate in the house for him and the children. He would occasionally pick up something himself, eating as they watched television and criticize her if she wanted some.

Gordon needed to maintain the relationship on this level so that whenever necessary he could storm out of the house in a towering rage, really relieved to get away to see his girl friend. Of course, he explained his need for Margaret through his unhappiness at home. He even suggested, "If it weren't for Margaret, my poor kids, whom I love more than anything, might be without their father today. I don't know if I could stand it if it wasn't for her."

Gordon never came back after the third counseling session. When he discovered that the therapist felt his actions were not the only possible solution to the situation, he left, saying, "I know you mean well, doctor; I know you do. But I'm afraid you just don't understand. There's nothing else I can do. I've got my kids to think of." Poor man. He went to his mistress's bed—a martyr.

When the partners play their marital roles more fully, the inhibition that has been trained into them becomes more and more obvious. The man becomes more a husband-*father* than husband, while the woman becomes more a wife-*mother* than wife. This activates their earlier inhibitions. Though she is attractive, he is not very responsive to her. This occurs in her response to him, too. Each of them may turn to people outside the marriage, whether in actuality or fantasy.

The separation of sex from love may appear clearly in the teenager's sexual relations. These are sometimes impersonal, even cynical. Teenagers may relate to their partners as *things* and not become emotionally involved. This emotional detachment may be the only way they can become aroused. But this attitude will come back to haunt them once they marry. Though at first they are very aroused by their spouse, as one becomes the husband-father and reacts to the other as the wife-mother, they become inhibited. They cannot overcome the long years of separating sex from love. Of course, many teenagers experience feelings of intense love in their sexual relations. This may be due to the fact that conditions within the home were such that sex did not become so negatively toned for them.

People must wean themselves of dependence on their parents before they can interact closely in marriage. They may be independent enough to carry out adult roles and responsibilities, but they must be *interdependent*—able to transfer a close relationship from their parents to their partner. This relationship must be built on trust and dependence on the other as *a primary source of love and affection.*

Those who can effectively express their sexual and affectional needs toward their partner typically have certain qualities. They carry out the marital roles—sexual, vocational, parental, social, companionship—without any undue stress that might deny their partner true satisfaction. They live in the here and now yet combine this approach to daily life with goals that are important to them. They are aware, authentic, valuing their own growth as well as that of their partner. They are capable of accepting criticism and changing. They communicate in a manner that is free of distortion so that they feel known and shared. Because they understand their partner, they are acceptant enough to adapt to many of their differences. They not only have the inner resources to enjoy themselves, but, secure enough to allow others to bring enjoyment to their partner, they do not feel that one is sexually or psychologically unfaithful when he or she enjoys the company of the opposite sex. They grasp what experience means to their spouse so that their behavior is centered in the other's needs as well as their own. They can be passive in love when to allow themselves to be given to is the way that they themselves can be the most giving.

One of the major reasons people get married to begin with is to have sexual relations regularly. Yet their interest sometimes fails to remain centered on their partner for very long. With the boredom of familiarity, they may become indifferent to each other and fail to avail themselves of the many sexual opportunities that arise within the home. Their mutual boredom causes resentment that poisons the relationship or disrupts it altogether. Novelty, on the other hand, makes for arousal; each is dismayed to discover how sexual he or she can feel as dormant sexuality is released in the excitement of a new contact. Their response may overcome age, color, or morals. Their sexuality is so urgent that they may respond intensely to any desirable person they pass on the street.

So it is not surprising that a man yearns for the good old days when he was a bachelor and was free to pursue women. A little apartment of his own, intimate dinners, cocktails, and then the seduction—such fantasies obsess him. Each mistress, he pictures, would be much sexier than his wife. And he will be as passionate with a mistress as he has always fancied he could be. He actually can be more lusty with other women, at least for a while. He shares only a limited part of his life with them, relating only as a sexual partner, so they do not activate his inhibitions as his wife does. And he terminates the relationship whenever difficulties arise. He becomes more aroused when he does not have to fear that his sexual response will commit him too deeply. Meanwhile, his arousal due to the newness of the other person temporarily gives him the feeling that he is *alive* again. His superficial involvement is a temporary bulwark against the aloneness of which he has become so aware in his marriage.

Certain social changes today have made it more urgent for people to try to overcome boredom and combine sexual and affectional needs in one person. Cities are larger, more impersonal, and they alter rapidly, so that it is difficult to feel important in a community. They may be haunted by the fear of being alone and unloved in a world that is heedless and constantly changing. They feel more secure when they stand together with their partner. Their emotional relationship, carrying the burden of greater personal need in today's impersonal world, shapes their life more than formerly. Their partner is more *uniquely* necessary to them today. This influences their sexual arousal with one another, offsetting the loss in attraction due to their long years together.

If sexual fidelity is a problem in marriage, so is *psychological* fidelity. People want to be the principal or sole source of their partner's nonsexual satisfactions. Yet their partner may at times prefer to interact with others. The frustration that each feels because the other insists on being the principal or sole source of satisfactions prevents certain sides of their personalities from emerging. This situation prevails even in good marriages. The woman who suddenly comes alive when she plays piano duets with the man from next door, and then, when he leaves, lapses into dullness with her husband, may infuriate her husband. His security is threatened when someone else satisfies an important need in her, "turning her on," so to speak. However, he is more likely to feel this way if their relationship is a poor one, for then he may fear the development of a sexual affair out of the musical interest she shares with their neighbor.

Sexual infidelity in marriage is fairly common. Usually the partner who discovers it is deeply hurt, even though he or she may have been unfaithful or had such fantasies. A person's picture of himself as an interesting and attractive person may be threatened and sometimes shattered. He is usually so concerned with his hurt feelings that he wants to retaliate in some way. Instead, it would be better for both of them were he to try to understand the meaning of his partner's behavior. In many cases such behavior is not a rejection of him so much as it is an expression of his partner's need for variety and the feeling of coming alive.

When infidelity comes to light, if the partner who has been faithful remains in the marriage, he or she tends to think that heightened sexuality, better communication, or a greater interest in the roaming spouse's work, could hold the other's exclusive interest. But while such efforts may heighten response somewhat, fundamentally the unfaithful partner is expressing a separate part of nature *against which he or she may not have been trained too strongly*—the biological need for variety.

Those who indulge their need for variety may not realize that putting all their energies and attention into a single partner may yield a greater emotional return. Marriage may be imperfect, but other relationships may leave even more to be desired. It is true that it is difficult to keep marriage stimulating and satisfying. But this is true of all relationships that are sustained for a long time. So marriage calls for everything that the person can give if it is to be successful. When this idea is the basis for fidelity, marriage may be more satisfying. Though faithful, the person displays a zest that he or she cannot feel when afraid and merely conforming to what is expected.

The insecure person may overconform to the wishes and needs of a partner. One may become so absorbed in a partner's attitudes, values, and ways of doing things that it is difficult to feel oneself to be an individual. In time, such a person may feel as if he or she is so centered in the other that his or her own identity has been lost.

The following brief history illustrates how fear and conformity block the person's desire to relate to others. Beneath Richard's conformity lies a poor picture of himself and his fear of rejection. But what is most obvious is that he relates distantly. This is typical of the person who cannot involve his emotions fully with his partner, failing to combine his sexual and affectional needs in her.

Richard was one of those people in whom one sensed a sharp inner conflict. He was pale, with heavily ringed eyes and the look of the man who is alone and depressed. When he spoke, an occasional spark of feeling broke through the dullness of his monotone. Richard had intense feelings, but he was afraid to express them. Now thirty-eight, he had been married for ten years, but though he was unhappy in his marriage, he could not give it up. If he did, he would be even more alone.

Richard never talked to the young woman who sat at the same lunch table in the company cafeteria. He was convinced that she had noticed the marriage band that he wore. But he passed her the salt, and she passed him the sugar or the mustard when he needed it. Each realized that the other was as alert to his needs as if they were having lunch together. And they both knew that for over a week now they had been looking forward to lunch at that particular table.

The inevitable happened. As Richard was handing her the sugar bowl one day, it slipped and clattered on the glass table top. This momentous event was all that was required to break their silence. In the days that followed, they told one another all about themselves, and the bonds between them grew stronger.

Finally, having learned where she lived, Richard called on her one evening without having arranged it beforehand. She welcomed him so effusively that it was clear even to him that she hoped for more. But he could not make any move toward her sexually. He enjoyed the evening so much that he repeated it several times. But though their friendship continued for some time, on no occasion did Richard even so much as touch her hand. Unconsciously, he used the relationship with her to strengthen his neurotic defenses against needing his wife too much. His very partial way of interacting with his "lover" was all that he dared risk with any woman.

It is difficult work to prepare one's self for marriage. Training at home, contacts with children, and being sexually uninhibited all help, however. A well-adjusted personality and relationships that foster maturity also help. But these contribute only a little to marital capacity. All one's life one is influenced to become married, yet hardly is prepared for the roles to be played. As a matter of fact, one is trained in various ways that oppose marriage. The dependence of prolonged adolescence, sexual inhibition, and the exploitative attitudes that develop so readily in our competitive culture hinder the emergence of an active love.

How can two people know they are in love in a way that is geared to the major challenge of marriage? When they respond to many of each other's *non*sexual qualities in such a way that they react sexually because of them; when they continue to feel good about the prospect of sharing their whole lives; when they want to help each other fulfill themselves and realize their goals in life; when they want to have children together; when they find companionship, stimulation, understanding, and acceptance with each other; when they share basic values yet accept the differences between them, and when the romantic element in their love is present but minimal—under these conditions, they are likely to combine their sexual and affectional needs effectively.

Many an unhappy person has wondered why a courtship that seemed so full of promise should have turned into such a dull marriage. Did he or she choose a spouse by sheer chance? Baffled and unhappy, they are inclined to think so. But the choice was not made by chance. Many unconscious factors caused them to select a particular person, and some of them were immature. Also, sexual attraction probably confused his or her judgment.

People find meaning in life in different ways. What a person gets excited about and strives toward tells a great deal about him or her. Whatever it is that creates meaning for him reflects his system of values, outlook on life, and level of maturity. A young woman may feel enhanced when she is seen in an expensive car, dressed "to kill," betting large sums at the racetrack, or dining in expensive restaurants. This tells us what gives meaning to her life, even though such meaning may not last very long. On the other hand, she may feel that her life would be exciting if she could communicate openly and freely with her partner. She would like to express her interest in social issues, she would like to have children, and she would like to cultivate sports and various cultural hobbies.

Yet she may drift into a relationship with a man who is not at all concerned about social issues. He prefers poker to sports, shows no interest in music, literature, theater, or art, is reluctant to have children, and refuses to discuss their personal life or express his feelings about it.

Two people who are so different may attract one another at first because of their loneliness. They may appeal to one another physically and sexually. They may need the partially shared life that each provides for the other. But she may soon realize that their relationship cannot provide excitement for her once she is no longer so lonely. The physical pleasure and the sharing that he provides do not make up for her frustration at not being able to talk to him about anything that really matters to her. That she is not a mother may leave her empty. Her activities no longer revolve around cultural interests, sports, or awareness of the social scene. She feels dull and bored. There must be common elements in what makes life exciting and meaningful to married people, otherwise they have to seek meaning separately.

It would seem that all too often people are more prepared for courtship than for marriage. They are trained in how to *get* married, that is, in the activities of courtship, but not in how to *be* married. Romantic and marital love have so little in common that one cannot judge the spouse by the lover. Still, the aim of courtship is usually marriage, and one makes a romantic choice that must serve in marriage.

When a marriage reaches the point at which the relationship no longer creates meaning for the partners and the way they interact fails to fill their needs, it may be because they are caught up in *neurotic dovetails.*

A neurotic dovetail exists when two people interact immaturely so that each brings out the other's immature behavior. Most of this kind of interaction takes place on an unconscious level. A young man may relate to his wife as a son, while she reacts to him mainly as a mother figure. He depends on her to look after him, make decisions, and take final responsibility for things. She dominates the relationship and unconsciously keeps it a distant one. She does not relate to him sufficiently as the seductive female because she doubts that she is attractive enough to hold his interest as such.

Another type of dovetail occurs in the couple who must always make a fine appearance. Their physical attractiveness, the smart level of their clothes, automobile, the places at which they eat, and the people with whom they associate are all essential to their feelings of adequacy. Any detail that mars the picture they cultivate disturbs them. Often they branch out into intellectual and cultural activities, too.

After two persons have been married for a while, they find that their dovetail becomes a source of friction. The mothering spouse becomes frustrated as a wife, while the submissive husband wants to assume more authority and responsibility. But, caught up in their dovetail, they discover that *desire is distinct from capacity.* While they wish to give up their mutual maneuvers, they find it very difficult to do so. And the harmony of the dovetail is only temporary. It is achieved by denying certain needs. Sustained harmony can rest only on the free expression of these needs. Since this is beyond the capacity of such a couple, the initial stability of their interaction crumbles.

The neurotic dovetail cannot survive the uneven growth of the partners. One of them may mature much more than the other. The immature partner then resists change in the more mature one. His interactive style is keyed to her *as she was.* In order to keep pace with her as she changes, he would have to mature himself. But neurotic dovetails stifle the person's growth. A young couple may have agreed that they would not have any children. She is afraid of the responsibility, and he wants to devote all his time and money to making his mark in the world. But after a while, feeling insecure, she would like to bind him to her by having several children. If he refuses, the harmony of their dovetail gives way to intense conflict.

Two partners are usually locked into a neurotic dovetail when they avoid the customary marital roles. The husband may refuse to assume financial responsibility for his wife and children. Or, he may assume these obligations in a very grudging way. He may relate to her sexually very seldom. He deprives both himself and her of any satisfaction from his performance of these roles. He uses the marital relationship as a cover-up for his basically withdrawn personality. The meaning that marriage provides for him is minimal. Donald is a good example.

Donald had developed the knack of giving the impression, through the mention of a name or a phrase, that he had read everything worthwhile that had ever been written. Myrna was the perfect foil for him. She listened, agreed, admired, and on occasion even worshiped. Regarding herself as inferior to Donald, she felt flattered at being his wife—and he knew it! She was content to admit his superiority whenever it pleased him to proclaim it. At least this was how things were on the surface.

Whatever Myrna's inner thoughts and feelings may have been, no one (least of all Donald) ever knew them. Sometimes she tried to break through to him. She would become silent, even depressed, and mutely plead for understanding. Her silence only made things worse, for Donald tolerated silence poorly. It was filled with unspoken thoughts, with deep feelings, and perhaps with unhappiness. So he would launch upon a discussion of anything that came to mind, always in his learned manner. But all it ever amounted to was a kind of false communication that prevented the expression of sincere feelings and kept their relationship superficial. This was the only way that Donald could deal with his stress when unspoken thoughts clamored for expression. Though Myrna was frustrated by his unconscious tactics, she also welcomed them. They pulled her out of her slump by sheer dint of verbal gymnastics. But afterward she hated him for them. Their dovetail lay in the way her inexpressiveness fitted in with his talkativeness and had been an important factor in their choice of one another.

As a result of their neurotic dovetails, two partners may become hostile and sexually bored with one another. They may have passed the point where working out their problems is feasible. Divorce is constructive when their ability to change and adapt is extremely limited.

Though a greater percentage of the population is married today, this leaves much to be desired as a measure of personal happiness. Couples may stay together, but this does not mean they have successfully combined their sexual and affectional needs in one another. They would feel humiliated in making a public confession of their failure, particularly in their social circle. Also, they have become so dependent on the *structure* that marriage gives their lives that it is difficult for them to give up the meaning that this structure represents. They fear being single and alone. They shrink from having to seek out a new partner, from choosing and being chosen for the second time. This is especially hard for those who are not inclined toward the "swinging" activities involved in courtship. Divorce is particularly hard for the woman older than thirty who has not yet had children and desires them. Her reproductive years are limited. And many people unconsciously are afraid to violate the lingering social standard that divorce is somehow a bad thing.

Many husbands and wives, though generally unhappy, are reluctant to give up the qualities in the other that they like. They hesitate to be without a sexual partner, for fear that, sexually driven, they may start relationships that are unsuitable for them and should never be begun. The wife often agrees with her husband that it is best for all concerned that he not be separated from the children. Some people do not want to give up the appearance of mature emotional adjustment that they feel marriage gives them.

When two people get divorced they are admitting that their marriage is not providing the rewards they had hoped for. But one of them may have grown within the marriage. If he or she has outgrown the neurotic dovetails into which they were locked, divorce may be a wise step. At least that partner may be capable of having children, good sexual relations, love, and companionship with somebody else. The partner who divorces in order to become an equal or to have a close relationship is maturing. Or one may divorce a spouse who refuses to have children in order to remarry and have children with someone else. Such a spouse is likely to have a good self-image. This person has the capacity to stand alone for awhile and the resources to relate closely to a new partner. If a marriage has been marked by passive, withdrawn interaction, one shows more maturity in getting a divorce than in remaining married.

Chapter 6

Values

The values that people develop within the home and in society help make their life meaningful. These values influence their behavior, their choice of goals, and the issues with which they become involved. They try to please those from whom they seek love by living up to their values. Carrying out values is also essential to a favorable picture of oneself. Of course, under certain circumstances they may not be able to do so.

It is fairly easy to find meaning in a society where tradition specifies how a person is to act. His or her values are simple enough, and they agree with those of everybody else. But our society is made up of different cultural groups, each with its own values. People belong to a number of these groups at the same time and must adhere to values that often conflict. The decisions that are the outcome of these conflicts may strain them to the breaking point. Their anxiety and depression demonstrate that they do not find their lives meaningful when their values are so conflicting.

They may feel compelled to give money to charity, even though they are not particularly well off. They may be opposed to force and violence, yet they kill others in their patriotic roles as soldiers. They deny themselves sexual outlets that are available to them. They resist the temptation to steal when they have great need of money. They save for the future, though they are tempted to indulge themselves in the present. They thus create meaning in their lives by adhering to their values. They organize their lives in a way that seems right to them, though if they are narrow and rigid in their thinking, their way may seem to be the *only* right way.

Once their values are clear, people are likely to have a satisfying feeling about who they are. They know what they stand for and where they want to go. Their values make up a large part of the individualities that set them apart from other people. These values give their lives order and direction. This is not true, of course, to the extent that their values conflict *within themselves*. A person may be homosexual and deeply ashamed of his sexual orientation, desiring nothing more than to be heterosexual. He or she may believe in marital fidelity and insist that a partner abide by the same code—yet be tormented with such desire for another that relating sexually to the spouse is no longer possible. A man and woman may regard sex as one of the most enjoyable of human experiences, only to discover that their guilt prevents them from enjoying it.

Many people value fairness and concern for others. Their concern with material things, however, may lead them to take advantage of others to gain their ends. They compete fiercely with others and employ tactics that violate their complimentary picture of themselves. Responsive to the lure of the advertising media, they may be unable to give up various luxuries yet are unable to take care of the basic needs of their families. They may love their parents and want to take care of them in their old age yet be frustrated because they do not have the financial means to start their own families with ones they love. They may believe in racial and religious equality yet find that they do not wish to have certain people for friends because of their color or religion. A man may insist that women should have complete equality with men yet discover that he is comfortable only with the woman who allows him special privileges and caters to him, subordinating herself. Though certain people may feel they can think things out for themselves, they may be ill at ease when their views do not fit in with those of the majority. Their resulting inability to be open and expressive may cause them to sacrifice their sincerity and spontaneity.

People may have certain points of view that do not fit in with prevailing legal and social codes. They may favor capital punishment, when the prevailing view regards it as "cruel and unusual." They may resent paying taxes, regarding the income tax law as having too many loopholes to be fair to the lower income groups. They may reject war as a means of resolving national differences and demand that the government adopt a more friendly attitude toward foreign powers. They may object to their country interfering in the internal affairs of other nations, regarding such policies as attempts to justify military expenditures that favor big business and the power of the military. If a man refuses to comply with a military draft, society may brand him an unpatriotic coward, a lawbreaker, and a selfish person who wants all the benefits of government without being willing to go out and fight for them and perhaps die. And it may slap him in jail, unless he flees the country first.

The homosexual may be so completely conditioned to his sexual preference that he cannot live in any other way; yet, if confronting the vice squads of larger cities he insists on his rights to be homosexual, he until recently has been regarded as abnormal and immoral. Believing in a democratic heritage, certain people may object to the economic and political power of the privileged minority. Asserting their right to speak freely, they are often silenced. They may feel at odds in these situations not only with society but, having adopted society's values to some extent, also with themselves.

One of the most important values of human beings is their emphasis on self-development and creativity. Their need to develop themselves is innate. Their creativity is part of this innate force. They may be creative when they express certain values against opposition. Or their creativity may appear in the new way they combine ideas. They produce books, paintings, musical compositions, inventions, and architecture. But it is the growth process itself, rather than its outcome in a concrete product, that tells of their creativity.

It may be true that for society to exist, the individual must conform to it. But it is also true that we need creative nonconformists who break new ground. The person's need to belong may influence him to conform to the standards and values of various groups. He or she may sacrifice creativity to fit in with others. But if creativity is an openness to experience, we cannot be very creative when we deny *our* experience and conform to that of others. We must be able to stand alone when necessary.

Many people are reluctant to express their emotions. They think of emotion as disruptive. While this may be true in certain situations, it is by no means generally so. Expressiveness is essential to creativity. Far from indicating a loss of control, expressiveness is balanced by restraint that has developed as a result of social and family training. Even personal relationships offer an opportunity to be creative, once creativity is understood to include reacting to a situation with individual attitudes, thoughts, and feelings.

Many people think that only the chosen few who possess a special ability are creative. Actually, everybody is creative or could be. The core of the person's creativity is that he meets experience with a fresh, inquiring mind, prepared to let it lead him wherever it will. He refuses to react in terms of prevailing ideas, notions, prejudices, beliefs, and stereotypes. These would prevent him from reacting in his own unique way. His creativity keeps him comfortable with himself as an always changing and broadening person.

Those who are creative maintain an open mind. They may stand by an earlier conviction or change it when new facts justify doing so. They are concerned neither with conforming to prevailing opinion nor with deviating from it but with responding to the factual or logical basis for acting. They respect established ways of thinking, but they do not revere them as the last word on the subject. Their reactions to any situation depend on their own values and criteria. They have a sense of *becoming*, and this makes their lives more meaningful. However, it cannot be said that those who are creative are always happy. But those who are uncreative are typically bored and depressed, with a negative outlook on life. They bog down in conformity, convention, and "safe" behavior.

Though creativity is not the special province of the chosen few, some people value it more highly than others. They make a greater effort to release and develop it. This may appear in the ways they teach school, organize a filing system, set up a real estate development, present a legal defense, or formulate a sales approach. The creative quality of these activities springs from the person's readiness to respond in an original way.

The child's behavior, shaped by a *child's* values, differs from that of the adult. The originality of his behavior may not be appreciated by the adult because an adult tends to evaluate it on the basis of adult standards. Also, the adult is likely to regard his own specific behavior as the measure of what is desirable.

All too soon the creativity of many children is stamped out as a result. The questions they ask may be answered on so elementary a level that their inquiring mind starves. Their parents do not take time for the child's groping and wondering. They may not respond to all that is exciting to him or her. They impose solutions on the child rather than allow him to search for answers that further excite and broaden his mind. There is some evidence to indicate that when parents show respect for a child, the child will express himself or herself creatively and not destructively. Such parents grant a great deal of freedom in making decisions and expect independence. They relate to their offspring in a liberating way and avoid being overly protective. Yet they do not reject the child. They also stress the development of the child's own ethical code so that he applies himself creatively to problems involving morality, justice, and fair play.

Unfortunately, the school system may play an important part in stifling the child's creativity. The size of classes and the emphasis on routine memorization in some schools block it. Repeating the mistakes of many parents, teachers may not permit him to develop his own solutions to problems. Such teachers may be bored, rigid, and fail to understand what it is that releases creativity. They may demand so much discipline and conformity that the child has little opportunity to organize experience in his or her own ways.

Society also grinds the creativity out of many adults who might otherwise cling to the little they have. The worker may have to perform the same limited task over and over. Charlie Chaplin's film *Modern Times* shows the deadening effect of mechanized, assembly-line production on the worker. In the end it reduces him almost to a robot. Also, the financial insecurity that haunts so many people produces anxiety and frustration unfavorable to the person's creativity.

A person may, however, make up for feelings of inadequacy by becoming very creative in a certain area. But this is not to imply in any way that one is generally dependent on emotional immaturity to be creative, a point of view that has been proposed by various writers. The lives of too many productive people who seem to have been quite mature negate this view.

Are men and women equally creative? Are they creative in different ways? These questions take on added importance in light of the current women's liberation movement. By and large, women have shown a recreative rather than an originally creative capacity, except in the writing of novels. Traditionally, women have been expected to follow in the footsteps of men and have been discouraged from showing leadership and breaking new ground. As a result, few women of the wealthy middle class, though they had been trained and educated, could think themselves as capable of original creative activity as men. But to the extent that the modern woman sees herself in a new light and expresses herself fully, she will be much more creative than those who went before her.

However, the creativity of women may take directions different from those of creative men, and perhaps women will employ different standards to evaluate their creative behavior. Interestingly, the way the sexes express themselves may be influenced by certain *physical* differences between them. Men have about a third more "vital capacity" (a measure of energy and stamina). This is reflected in oxygen delivery to various parts of the body, including the brain. But the main physical difference that affects creativity may be the male sex hormone. There is some reason to believe that the driving force, aggressiveness, initiative, persistence, and exploratory activity of men are due in large part to the secretion of this hormone.

Certainly such qualities are important in any type of original work, especially in larger creations, since the person must have the physical capacity to persist until completion. These qualities are probably just as important in setting up a project, too. This calls for the daring and initiative to combine things or ideas in the new ways that are so typical of the creative person.

Chapter 7

The Achievement Neurosis

Achievement plays a dominant role in our culture. Nothing reveals the basic values of people more clearly than their attitudes toward it. They may *profess* certain values that are consistent with the Judeo-Christian ethic and with a tradition of democratic fair play, but their desire to achieve may bring out entirely different values in them.

People take on a succession of roles as they mature. These organize their lives in a way that makes them feel that they are a part of society. Meanwhile, depending on how they carry out their roles, they express their particular values in regard to them.

But what of the person who fails to take on new roles? Unconsciously, he may set out to make up for his failure *through some type of achievement*. This displaced behavior is neurotic. Any activity, behavior, or goal, normal in itself, may be put to this neurotic use.

It is not the achievement in any special activity that is neurotic *in and of itself*. It is important to separate normal achieving behavior from that meant to make up for a person's inadequacies, and this will be discussed more fully later. Achievement is neurotic only when people use it *in place of an area of frustration*. They may try to make up for their sexual inhibition or their conviction that they are of a faith, color, or economic class that has little status. What is common to all these situations is that people rely on their achievement for the sense of worth that they should get from other sources.

The person may try to become an outstanding athlete, a noted doctor, or a successful businessman. He may adopt a style of life that carries status with it, such as "smart" suburban living. He may pursue intellectual and cultural activities. Many men and women emphasize their physical and sexual allure. They create a picture of a successful personal and emotional life, playing the dating game and passing through a series of affairs. But though they do not really share themselves with their partners, this is their particular form of achievement.

The achievement neurotic typically applies himself excessively in one area. He hopes, often unconsciously, that his achievement will *indirectly* satisfy needs and goals that would be overwhelming were he to actually try to deal with them. He is encouraged in this by a society that applauds achievement no matter what motivates it. But after he has succeeded in athletics, in a profession, or in business, he may find that his achievement never makes up for the needs that he put aside originally. He discovers certain roles to be so basic that unless he carries them out he remains emotionally adrift. He realizes that he has been running and running on a treadmill of substitutive adequacy that gives him no feeling of worth. His success may have brought him relationships of love and friendship, but his capacity for these has remained undeveloped during his pursuit of achievement. His success doesn't give his life much additional meaning at all.

But long before he realizes this, *achievement has be-*

come a primary value for him. It has wormed its way into his life, giving direction to his goals, his activities, and even his moral outlook. His need for *direct personal fulfillment* is submerged in the striving through which he hopes to feel adequate. He is convinced that he can have both his achievement and the other satisfactions that he expects to gain through it. And on the surface, he may seem to have both. But he gains only the form of the personal satisfactions he seeks, not their spirit.

It is not difficult to understand how a person falls into this trap. Our culture demands that achievement precede personal fulfillment. As a result achievement has become a basic value. Since its outer appearance is as varied as the texture of American life, it disguises a great deal of emotional immaturity and frequently is not detected as a neurosis. It may take an *active* form, as when the person organizes activity and accomplishes something, or it may take a *passive* form, in which he or she is very dependent on some minor skill for a sense of worth. One may also emphasize future achievement, which is somehow always elusive. Sometimes the passive form is based on pure fantasy, as in the case of the mechanic who thinks of himself as a writer but never writes.

The achievement neurosis is built around a person's picture of him or her self. Let us see, then, what the impact of our type of society has been on the way individuals see themselves.

In societies organized on a communal basis or around feudalism or slavery, the person's self-picture was overshadowed by the idea of the group. An individual was not even responsible directly for the necessities of life. Unless one belonged to the ruling class one was not very important. Rigid codes guided behavior; each person knew his humble place in the scheme of things. The society was centered on the needs of the group as a whole or the wishes of the ruling minority. There was little room for taking the lead, for growth, or for achievement, so the person was passive. In Russia and China today, depending on their stage of development, the group may be more important than the individual.

But gradually the emphasis shifted from the group to the person. Leading thinkers of the twelfth and thirteenth centuries, for example, emphasized the importance of the individual's feelings, ideals, goals, and suffering. Slavery was later abolished in some parts of the world and finally in the United States. The right of kings to rule the common man was challenged. The criminal and the insane were treated more humanely. The feminist movement argued for the equality of women and men, so that relatively recently the vote was extended to women. Even more recently the voting age has been lowered. During the past 150 years the political, social, and economic opportunities and privileges of the average person have been extended greatly.

All these changes focused on *the individual as the important unit of society*. They reflected a growing concern for his welfare and in general gave him greater control over his fate. His picture of himself became more important to him, for as his rights were broadened so were the demands made on him. He had to live up to these to feel good about himself. Meanwhile, the tightly knit family of parents and children became more common. The child now occupied the attention of parents to a much greater extent than formerly. So he became quite self-centered, continuing to value himself as he grew to adult years. No longer given to subordinating himself to the group, he felt it was up to him to develop his potential. His effort to do so often disguised his immaturity, as he substituted achievement for a general sense of worth.

Our industrial system puts pressure on the person to follow some particular line of work—doctor, lathe operator, teacher, carpenter, or whatever. The system is dependent on specialization and the division of labor. The Jack-of-all-trades who is master of none no longer fits in too well. The person's status and worth depend on being able to do some particular kind of work. When group participation was emphasized, the laborer was unable to identify fully with the product of his efforts. *He has just as much difficulty doing so today.* As a rule, he neither owns the tools of production nor has much to say about what he will help make with them. He becomes a nameless cog in the vast and impersonal wheel of our industrial machine. It is hard to take personal pride in the making of things when one is so unimportant in planning or finishing them. Yet most people spend the major part of their days at work. No wonder it is difficult for an individual to have a satisfactory picture of himself.

On industrialism's brighter side, the steady decrease in working hours has given the person a chance to develop himself more fully in other directions. If his work reduces him to a robot, he can offset this by developing himself through his personal activities. Such opportunities are greater today than ever before. Wages, hours, fringe benefits, and leisure time are all more favorable. One is likely to have a good picture of himself if he is satisfied that he has used his opportunities well, but he may be dissatisfied if he feels he has not. But even when his abilities are considerable, he may feel inadequate. This occurs when he turns to achievement to offset the frustration arising from other areas. Then his achievement must satisfy not only his need for status, but it must also gain for him a beautiful wife, love, children, and a fine home. But he is unlikely to have the personal resources to interact effectively when he finally achieves these, so that he fails to live meaningfully through his family.

A woman, too, has a much better opportunity today to develop her potential. Industrialism's technology enables her to perform household tasks with much less expenditure of time and energy. Interestingly, although until recently the achievement neurosis occurred predominantly among men, today the emerging woman, as she becomes involved in the world outside the home, may find herself increasingly subject to this neurosis.

Many people come to feel that so much depends on their achievement that they may lower their ethical standards. In competing with others they may gain some advantage through tricky practices that are barely within the law. They hardly hesitate to undercut a competitor or friend. Our society values achievement so highly that it often ignores the methods the person uses. This dog-eat-dog approach, which makes the possession of wealth the highest virtue, filters through to all levels of society. The person ranks others according to it, shrinking or inflating their worth according to the size of their bank account.

Loosely speaking, in the United States we have a lower class, a middle class, and an upper class. These divisions are geared to income, but other qualities that derive from wealth separate the classes, too—amount of leisure time, education, cultural interests, marriage customs, morals, employment of servants, nature of hobbies, opportunity to vacation abroad, choice of automobiles, size and location of home, type and quality of clothes, and many other things about the person's life-style.

Now the wealthy minority is ordinarily not a striving group. And the lower-income working class is occupied with earning a living in routine jobs. So it falls to the middle class to produce the professional people on whom the operation of our complex society depends. The middle class is wealthy enough to live beyond the necessity of worry, yet not wealthy enough to live off accumulated capital. It regards hard work as virtue. It values highly both education and striving for a better life. The achievement neurosis occurs mainly among the artistic, intellectual, professional, commercial, and business members of this class—in the active form. It occurs among many others in the passive form.

People must achieve if they are to supply their families with the good things in life—living in a respectable neighborhood, an education, expert medical care, an interesting vacation, and many others. Only then can they feel that they belong. The picture of the good life that the communication media keep before them is filled with material things. They feel they must struggle to achieve so they can have these things. They cannot be expected to resist values that disguise their inadequacies so well. They usually anticipate that they will turn to their personal roles and the satisfaction of their needs at a later time. But they have so formed their personalities that they will find it hard to do so effectively.

The achievement neurotic is almost always sexually inhibited. Historically, sex has been inhibited in the United States. The reasons have varied with the moral outlook of the times, the influence of orthodox religion, knowledge of contraception, population needs, the desire to preserve the home and marriage, and economic factors. But today the inhibition of sex is more and more coming to be linked with achievement. The inadequate person, feeling hopeless about being loved for himself, presents his achievement as the basis for others to accept and love him. Meanwhile, until he is successful, he remains withdrawn, his sexual drive inhibited. He hopes to barter his status and wealth for acceptance, love, and sex, and it is true that his achievement brings these within his reach.

He justifies his inhibition by the necessity to set aside his sex drive if he is to devote himself to developing his specialized skills and abilities. While his inhibition pushes him on toward achievement, his achievement makes him more attractive sexually. He becomes someone to be sought for marriage. But once he tries to enjoy the benefits that led him to achieve in the first place, he finds that he can do little more than go through the motions. He may be demanding sexually, but this reflects his need for *reassurance* more than his uninhibited sex drive.

The person who has ignored his needs for sex and love for a long time has cut grooves of withdrawal and self-centeredness deeply into his personality. The aggressive qualities that he develops in striving for achievement are opposed to the giving that is the core of love. This withdrawal and self-centeredness occur less in the woman than the man because achievement is not as commonly one of her main goals. This difference is starting to disappear today under the influence of the women's liberation movement.

The achievement neurotic offers passive rather than active love to his partner. He fails to satisfy her needs for sex, love, and understanding *directly* but hopes to win her favor indirectly through his achievement. He does not feel worthy because of how he walks, talks, thinks, or because of his values and the roles he plays, and his concept of himself is poor. He thinks he must be unique in some way before he can make up for his overall feelings of inadequacy. He does not *interact* with his partner so much as gain reassurance of his worth through his *possession* of her. As a result, it is hard for him to believe in whatever acceptance and love she may give him. This is why he feels so alone even when he is surrounded by those who are trying to love him.

He is given to masturbation, fantasy, and a preoccupation with the sexuality that he cannot express. When he has intercourse he never really loses himself in it. He often feels more like an observer than an actual participant. His sexual problems, originally due to guilt and inhibition, are added to by the withdrawn quality of the relationship, which is all that he can tolerate.

All achieving behavior is not unconsciously intended to make up for a person's inadequacies. In and of itself, the desire to achieve is by no means neurotic. It may simply be part of the person's innate drive to realize his potential. People value achievement not only as a means to other goals but *as an end in itself*. They are involved in it because of its own appeal and not simply because of its rewards.

Achievement may fail to appear as one of the person's chief drives, either for some time or perhaps never. But this does not mean that the drive is not innate. By way of comparison, the sexual drive does not become intense until a person is about thirteen. He or she may not even be able to express it for many years after that, yet it is undeniably innate.

The person who expresses an innate need to achieve in a normal way tends to enjoy his daily work. His productivity appears in other sides of his life, too. As a rule his close relationships are rewarding and fulfilling. He is typically expressive in them and has the capacity to satisfy his basic needs. He adapts to his environment without undue stress. He likes to feel that he has some standing in his immediate circle, and he almost always does. Achievement as a substitute for other drives that he cannot face and express is foreign to him.

Men and women who achieve normally tend to be *altruistic*, so that they may give time and energy to social problems. They may insist that the person who demands that proper measures be taken to guard the quality of air, water, and soil is more realistic than the achieving executive who puts corporate profits before the control of pollution. Altruism has become a primary source of meaning in a society where growing complexity threatens our very survival. Indeed, yesterday's altruism has become the stark necessity of today.

The generation gap that was so wide until recently has narrowed to some extent as young people have turned once again toward achievement. To the extent that their turning away was a revolt against neurotic striving, it was constructive. But in many cases this revolt arose from a person's failure to face his or her own incompetence. These young people tried to feel adequate through supporting a new set of values. That is, they defined themselves to be adequate. But many of their values failed to prepare them to satisfy basic needs—their own or those of anyone else. These values allowed them to live in limbo, as it were, a maneuver that was as neurotic as substitutive achievement. Today this type of defensive withdrawal from the establishment is much less evident. However, this is not to suggest that those young people who are at odds with the established order because they insist it live up to the ethical values it pretends to follow are behaving immaturely.

Unlike normal achievers, achievement neurotics seldom strive because of the activity itself. They derive little satisfaction from it. The achievement is what they seek.

Their need to be outstanding limits their activities to those in which they are likely to be superior. This is why they seldom become well-rounded people.

On the other hand, their need to be outstanding may cause them to pose as experts in fields where they are no more than novices. A familiar example is the successful businessman who is convinced that his political views are particularly astute. He regards himself as an authority on how to bring up children. He is convinced that his views on the stock market and on inflation should be listened to with great respect. Actually, his opinions may be elementary and uninformed. He may have no better claim to insight in any of these matters than the person with whom he disagrees so strongly. His unconsciously poor picture of himself is reinforced as he fails to get favorable feedback from those he tries to impress. He may doubt himself even in his special field of competence. Inevitably, he is sensitive to criticism of any kind.

We have already pointed out that the achievement neurosis occurs in two forms, active and passive. The active form occurs when the person has the capacity to achieve his goals. This may provide him with just enough feeling of adequacy to keep him chained to his substitutive achievement. But, like the man in the following example, he may have acute anxiety attacks.

At twenty-eight, Henry had many anxiety attacks. They were linked to humiliating and frightening experiences that he had had as a soldier. But they were also linked to his attempt to feel important and worthwhile as a civilian.

Henry was now in a safe environment and one in which he was treated with dignity and respect. But various stimuli—trucks, airplanes overhead, a fire engine, sirens, certain types of people, or a foreign accent—aroused his old fear of death. Innocent requests by his wife to wash the dishes, peel some potatoes, or clean up the bathroom seemed very humiliating to Henry. He reacted with anger, then with fear of his own anger; that is, of what he might do. Actually, he did nothing except hold it all in. These intense feelings brought on his attacks.

Henry had been a private in the service. He felt that he had been ordered about a great deal and treated shabbily. But now that he was a civilian again, he was determined to prove his worth and win the respect of his friends. He was prepared to work hard to do this. Yet, being out among people all the time exposed him to a number of situations that set off his acute anxiety attacks. But he had to be out in the world for he was a salesman by profession.

As an attack came on, Henry began to perspire in a cold, clammy way. He felt nauseous and sometimes had diarrhea. His vision blurred, he could feel the blood drain from his face, he became dizzy, and he felt that he was on the verge of fainting. At such times he had a terrible feeling of dread; yet felt utterly helpless to ward off the vague danger that menaced him. This acute type of attack would come on him suddenly. It may have been brought on by some trivial event that he could only half suspect had anything to do with it. It left him limp, exhausted, unable to present himself to anyone as the high-powered salesman he was.

Henry tried to deal with these attacks by avoiding the situations that seemed to trigger them. He was cautious, rigid, and tried to control the environment so that he could operate safely within it. But he found that the environment always seemed ready to spring some hidden trap on him. The drone of a plane, the grinding of a transmission gear, interaction with someone who had an accent, and Henry suddenly changed from a hard-driving salesman to a frightened child who wanted desperately to do only one thing—escape and hide somewhere.

Shortly after an attack, however, Henry's need to feel that he was a person of some importance drove him out of his isolation and toward his ambitious goals. As he ventured out of his shell, he exposed himself to the stimuli that triggered his attacks. His need to achieve and his unconscious fear of death and of his own anger were in a daily conflict that was the source of his acute anxiety attacks.

Henry could overcome his anxiety attacks by taking a number of steps. First, he would have to develop insight to their cause. Then, he could set about desensitizing himself to the stimuli that triggered them. This would call for placing himself in situations containing such stimuli at times when his anxiety was reduced by preparing for the situation or by having someone support him in it. Then, he could strengthen himself in those areas where his feelings of inadequacy led him to compensate through achievement. Finally, greater self-acceptance (to be distinguished from approval) would ease further his substitutive need to achieve.

The active achievement neurotic often is too sophisticated to develop symptoms of fantasy, make-believe, or game-playing; so he suffers a great deal of anxiety and depression. He is subject to stomach distress, insomnia, excessive perspiration, muscle tension, and other symptoms. In more severe cases, he may have an ulcer, asthma, or high blood pressure. He is engaged in a constant struggle to be what he thinks he should be in a society that, praising achievement and success, diverts him from satisfying his needs normally.

Many a person who is absorbed in substitutive striving does not succeed in some form of visible achievement. In the passive form, the person's sense of well-being is just as dependent on achievement as in the active form. But he or she succeeds in doing no more than fantasizing that he will become outstanding. He is forced to make much of small virtues. He expects his achievement to become real in the near or distant future, but it never does. He does not have the intellect or discipline to make it a reality. Nor does he have the capacity to judge his abilities realistically.

As the picture people have of themselves has become more complex, they have had to ignore more and more negative qualities in themselves to feel adequate. The more they do this, the more inaccurate their picture of themselves becomes and their ability to interact well with others becomes limited. They set goals for themselves that they cannot reach, thus showing the neurosis in its passive form.

The passive form occurs commonly in people who are overdependent in their important relationships. They want to be cared for completely. This desire to avoid the hectic, competitive pace of our society comes into conflict with their need to achieve. A number of paths are open. They may relate to someone in a clinging, passive way, or may remain withdrawn from relationships. Also, they may react to their desire for overdependence with such abnormal physiology that they develop a psychosomatic disease.

In psychosomatic ulcer, for example, usually the person develops the capacity to work toward goals effectively, showing the active form of the neurosis. This is also true of those who suffer intense anxiety attacks. Though they are apprehensive, they are driven toward their ambitious goals. But those with psychosomatic asthma or high blood pressure are likely to show the neurosis in its passive form. The person with high blood pressure resents the need to strive, and this prevents him from organizing his efforts. If the person has asthma he or she needs a strong figure to lean upon constantly and is too dependent to strive effectively.

It is easier to make progress in psychotherapy with the passive form of the neurosis. The person is not so locked into the neurosis through the rewards of actual achievement. But the passive achievement neurotic may turn to alcohol for relief from the depression arising from failure. In that case, drinking replaces actual achievement in giving a false sense of well-being. The passive achievement neurotic is then likely to have no more insight to focus on striving than does the successful, active achievement neurotic. And he or she proves to be just as resistant to treatment.

Chapter 8

Identity

It is difficult for people to find meaning in life unless they have a clear and favorable *identity*. They must see themselves as specific types of people in their social, work, and personal relationships. Without this secure sense of a satisfying self that is ever changing yet derives so largely from the previous self, they cannot know who they are, what they stand for, or where they are going.

This is particularly true whenever they face a period of change, for change tests the maturity and stability of their identity. When people who have been married for a long time are divorced, they may feel confused as to who they are. They may be unable to act freely as single persons especially if they are still linked indirectly to their former spouse through their children. Of course, "stability of identity" does not mean a fixed quality so much as it means being able to function while changing.

Each stage of development calls for a new identity. Those who are prepared for it make an *identity transition*; otherwise they show *identity confusion*. If their confusion is extreme, they may suffer an *identity crisis*. In that case, though they are unable to follow a new path, they can no longer remain on the old. They go back to a lower level of functioning, so that they cannot satisfy their needs as fully. If they are to find meaning in their lives, they must be ready to live each role in the here and now without distorting it and then progress to the next.

Identity transition, confusion, and crisis have usually been thought of as intensified during adolescence. Young people have been pictured as having great difficulty adapting to what society expects of them. Also, their physical and emotional needs are emerging rapidly at this time. This emphasis on adolescence may not be realistic today, a time in this country of rapid change in our entire outlook on life. Sexual patterns, ethnic relations, ecological values, attitudes toward patriotism and war, and the nuclear menace are changing society. As groping adolescents try to adapt to these influences, they are as perplexed as anyone else but probably no more so. The transitions that adults are called on to make are just as sensitive. The greater the social ferment, the greater the challenge to the person's identity—no matter what his or her stage of life. Sometimes adolescents who are not yet fixed in their ways may adapt even better than adults. So this discussion does not focus on the adolescent in particular.

The person's identity may be thought of as consisting of a number of subidentities. These vary in importance at different stages of life. To young adults of twenty-one, their *physical* identity is perhaps most important. They need to feel that they are attractive, perhaps even more attractive than average. If they are disabled in any way that can be seen, their physical identity is likely to weaken their identity as a whole. Physical identity is closely related to *sexual* identity. Is the person exciting to the opposite sex? Are they virile, passionate lovers? Unless they feel they are, their sexual side will not contribute to a positive identity.

To people in their thirties, other subidentities are likely to be important—among them intellectual identity. Our society has made the transition from what was largely a farming economy as late as 1900 (in which physical identity was very important) to the industrial-commercial-professional economy we have today. Those with emotional problems may depend on their intellect to make up for other sides of their identity with which they feel less secure. The professional man whose physical appearance is mediocre may marry an attractive woman of limited education. He offers his intellect and the style of life to which it leads, in exchange for her beauty. She offers her beauty in exchange for his intellect and the opportunity to move up in the social scale.

The person's *vocational* identity carries with it a certain amount of status. It is one thing to be a gas meter reader, a garbage collector, or a house painter; it is another to be a lawyer, doctor, or businessman. The person's income fixes the style of his life. This is reflected in his choice of automobile, the size and location of his house, the vacations he takes, and the other ways he spends his money.

But it is difficult for a person to derive status from vocational identity, no matter what it may be, if he cannot feel directly related to the product of his work. Unless he is a professional man in private practice, an independent businessman, or an independent manual worker, his contribution to the final product may be barely visible. This is a serious problem in the United States today. While it has been discussed elsewhere in the context of work being meaningful, I wish to emphasize it here in relation to the person's sense of identity.

Vocational identity is related to the person's *role-playing* identity. As provider for the family, the man must have a dependable, respectable job and an adequate income. In addition, he must have the maturity and personal qualities that are essential to taking on new roles—husband, sexual partner, parent, companion, person of cultural interests—as he progresses through the various stages of life. As homemaker, the woman must be a loving and understanding mother and wife, a warm companion, and skillful in the management of the home. As her children become grown she may function vocationally outside the home, or she may choose to do so while they are still quite young.

As people turn forty, what might be called *institutional* identity takes on added importance. They become more aware of the rapidity with which the years pass, and they cling to a sense of affiliation with their country, the armed forces, a trade union, the political party of their choice, or their religion. The language as spoken in their part of the country, and the locale with which they are familiar (including its style of dress), provide an unchanging backdrop of stability and security that lessens the threat of their own changing selves as they age.

These institutions contribute to a pride in belonging, which helps people feel their identity. Their sense of belonging depends on conformity to the customs, values, and traditions of the culture. No matter where they are, or how alone they may be, when they observe the tradition of Christmas or other holidays, for example, they feel part of what is continuous in the culture. As they move through time and a changing social order, they strengthen their identity by carrying something unchanging with them. They have observed these holidays all their lives. Their parents did so before them and they are teaching their children to do so. This may be what motivates the most humble official of the British foreign service to pay tribute to the Queen by wearing his uniform in the sweltering heat of some far-flung outpost. He creates a feeling of stability in a life that in a distant corner of the earth has been torn from its familiar roots. But *over*conformity weakens the person's identity, for then he or she is not directed from within enough to feel that he belongs to himself.

The *psychological* identity that people develop becomes more and more important in their search for meaning. Do they see themselves possessing the qualities that permit them to function as trusting, secure, well-adjusted people who esteem themselves? Or are they suspicious of others, hostile, with a negative outlook on life? Do they relate closely to those who are important in their lives? Can they satisfy their marriage partner's basic needs and allow their spouse to do the same for them? Are they really *with* their children when they are together?

Various factors influence the changing quality of people's identity. We have seen that at different stages the different subidentities vary in importance. These also vary in relation to their training, values, goals, and life history. Their identity is influenced, too, by how they feel others see them. But how others see them influences them *only within the setting of their own values*. These values filter the impact of others' reactions to them. And, as was suggested in the brief discussion of adolescence, the greater the change in the social scene, the greater stimulation to change in the person's identity.

Certain subidentities, such as role-playing, sexual, and psychological, remain more or less vague until the person becomes linked in a durable relationship. Then they crystallize. The emergence of psychological identity is seen clearly in the interaction of the child with his parents. As a developing child, he or she changes rapidly. Any failure on the part of the parents to recognize and adapt to this fluid nature blocks the crystallization of the child's psychological identity. This process continues until the children are grown and have left the home. At that point their psychological identities change sharply as they adapt to the new demands made upon them.

From this brief description of the various subidentities, it is obvious that overall identity, a combination of subidentities, plays an important part in the person's capacity to experience meaning in his or her life.

Modern society calls forth a complex identity in people by making many demands. It is not easy for them to develop a stable identity when their values are in conflict with one another. Yet they cannot avoid conflict when they are a member of several subcultures, each of them different.

Also, while society is changing its values rapidly in regard to the status and opportunities available to various ethnic groups, many members of majority groups resist such change. As a result, racial and religious factors make it hard for many members of minority groups to develop a stable identity. They try to enter those ranks that until recently seemed so superior and so unattainable, but they are not always welcome. They are understandably confused as to how much of their unique personal quality they should sacrifice in order to fit in.

Meanwhile, members of majority groups face new problems of identity, too. Are they the kind of people who could date a black, Jewish, Mexican-American, or Oriental individual? Should they bring the minority member into their family? Would this be harmonious with the way they see themselves fitting into society? Achieving a clear identity in this regard can be very hard when people have such a wide range of choices as today.

If society plays a formative role in the person's identity, parents exert an even more important influence during the early years. Until about seventy-five years ago, most Americans were small farmers or shopkeepers. Children spent a great deal of time with their fathers and mothers, helping them in their work. But today, in most cases, the father works away from home. As a result, the mother has become the dominant figure in the lives of her young children. Their father may earn the money to buy food and clothes, but the ice cream and toys that their mother allows them are more real to them. Her influence is increased as she acquires an ever greater share of society's wealth through inheritance and divorce settlements, for wealth means power. Once children have started school, they spend a great deal of time in the lower grades with what is usually a substitute "mother," the teacher, who often exerts a very important influence on their thoughts and behavior.

So it is not surprising that a male child finds it hard to model himself after the traditional male qualities. His father's absence and the resulting dominance of his mother may cause him to downgrade his father and *dis*identify with him. Unless he is fortunate enough to fix on a suitable substitute, this deprives him of a model for his future maleness. Also, it may lead to a confused picture of what a woman is if the mother—moving into the vacuum created by the father's absence and necessarily displaying certain of his masculine qualities—fails to show her feminine qualities sufficiently.

If this imbalance is to be overcome, both parents must become much more aware than they ordinarily are of the need children have to model themselves after them. The mother must take advantage of every opportunity to point out to the young child the behind-the-scenes importance in his or her life of the father who is away at work. She can do this effectively only if she herself has a basic respect for the father and his roles. She cannot do it if she stands between the father and child, funneling their interaction through herself. When the father asks the child to do something, the child may ask his mother, "Do I have to?" If she answers "yes" or "no," she strips the father of all authority in the child's eyes. Instead, her answer might be, "You heard what your father said. Don't ask me; just do it!" If the child asks information of the father and then asks the mother, "Is that right?" her answer might be, "Your father just answered you."

For his part, if the father is to do all that he can to model masculinity for his children, he must play an intimate part in their daily lives and help form their personalities. This may require him to make substantial changes in his daily routine and perhaps even in his life-style. In order to share in their personal care from the earliest days, he may have to rise earlier, not work overtime, and participate in family activities fully on weekends. Otherwise, he cannot hope to play an important part in his children's everyday problems and achievements. In addition, children need to observe how their mother and father relate as man and woman, if their own sexual identity is to emerge in mature form.

Some children develop homosexual tendencies. A father who is absent physically or emotionally, or a mother who is overprotective of her son, cannot be effective models. The child may fail to adopt the sexual identity that society expects of him. Of course, today, the homosexual is more likely to belong openly to the homosexual community and enjoy a sense of belonging within it. If a person responds sexually to men and women, the sense of belonging may be less than that of the person who is only homosexual. He may not be able to enter fully either the homosexual or the heterosexual community, remaining on the fringe of each. But he or she is no different from many people, homosexual or not, who also maintain emotional distance between themselves and others. Lewis, for example, was unable to resolve his fear of attaching himself closely to either sex.

At twenty, Lewis was poignantly conflicted in his sexual identity. He wanted very much to become a professional man, marry, maintain a home, and have children. This was how he had been trained. But his response to a girl was no more than lukewarm, and his entire heterosexual experience consisted of a few kisses. All his fantasies, often accompanied by masturbation, were about men. Yet he had never had sexual contact with a man, fearing to start a pattern of relationships that he would not be able to give up. Interestingly, he had never even had a crush on a specific man.

Lewis was constantly depressed by this problem. Yet he seemed unable to get rid of his homosexual fantasies or stop clinging to the heterosexual way of life. As a result, he felt isolated from males and females alike.

When they are comfortable with their changing selves, people have the capacity to move on to new levels of behavior. The flexibility to do this may become one of their most strongly held values. Certain areas of their growth depend on maturing physically, others psychologically. They change from being children at home who are loved because they are who they are, to children at school who are evaluated on the basis of what they can do; from the young boy or girl who lives in a sexual vacuum, to the adolescent who hardly knows what to do with his or her surging sexuality in our restrictive culture; from the college student who is expected to study and get through school, to the employee who must take responsibility for supplying his or her own wants; from the young single person who is concerned chiefly with achieving independence, to the young husband or wife on whom others depend; from the romantic lover in early marriage, to the husband or wife who must adapt to the needs of the family and show the capacity to meet its requirements.

An especially sensitive transition often occurs in the mid-forties, when people start to question their future. They probably must face the bleak fact that they are never going to achieve most of their ambitions and goals in their jobs or personal lives. They realize that they are no longer young enough to put in long years before they can enjoy the outcome of their efforts, and this destroys their ambition. Their capacity to hope and look to the future will most likely be severely tested in their mid-forties.

People look for meaning not only in the external world but also within themselves. They must always hold onto the core of their personalities. Yet, if they are to develop and grow, they must constantly reshape this core, reaching beyond themselves while preserving their essential personalities. Unless they maintain this delicate balance, they feel a loss of identity. This occurs, for example, when they become too much what others want them to be. When they overconform in this way, their lives lose meaning. They may then reduce their contacts with and their participation in groups. Their purpose is to regain their core by asserting greater control over what they want to do and think and feel. However, any immature behavior that they show as they try to do this has a constructive side in that it is not only a failure in adjustment but also helps them to preserve their identity.

The person may be reluctant to give up the secure lifestyle he or she already has mastered. All resources may be strained as he clings to an identity that is satisfying to him yet must remain open to change. He has a drive to not remain fixed; at the same time, he is afraid to meet the demands of growth. He may thus evade the anxiety of growing until he can tolerate it and make the transition. At first, *he moves away from what he does not want to be. Only then can he move toward what he wants to be.* Certain events such as starting kindergarten, maturing sexually at thirteen, graduating from high school, dating, marrying, taking on the provider role, and parenting jar him loose from his familiar and secure ways. The changes that he undergoes must be accomplished within a period of time that meets the expectations of both the culture and the person himself. Ultimately, if these changes have not been too stressful, they become part of his functioning self.

All things end. The ending of a phase of the person's life is contained in its beginning. Should he or she be unable to tolerate an ending and fail to make a necessary transition, he narrows the scope of his life. But the effective person adapts his identity to his ever-changing self. He makes the transition from the dependent adolescent to the self-sufficient adult. When the right moment has arrived, he may end a relationship that has deteriorated. He may refuse to adopt the submissive attitude that his boss demands of him, preferring to leave the company instead.

Some transitions call on people to change some of their values, and with them their style of life. For example, a woman may decide that she has been the swinging bachelor-girl long enough. She is no longer satisfied with her fine apartment, good income, and succession of boy friends who are willing to seduce her. She may be ready to relate more closely. To do so, she will have to give up being centered on herself and become accountable to her partner. Someday, when she takes on the parental role, her life-style will change further.

In each of the transitions that people make, they must be tuned to their emerging selves. They ally themselves with those parts of their changing selves with which they can be most effective and creative, giving up those they have outgrown. Even though they are comfortable and secure with certain roles, they may have to shed them for the broader selves that they hope to develop. Jane was unhappy because she had not been able to do this.

At forty, Jane was angry and disgusted with herself. Ten years earlier, she had wanted to take several courses at college. But she was unable to tolerate being a mere beginner and studying with younger people, for she was a college graduate. So she had put it off. Why be a beginner when she had already arrived as a wife, a mother, and the owner of a luxurious Buick? She already had status of a kind.

But now, still interested in academic subjects, Jane was as ignorant of them as ever and as frustrated. Only now it seemed even harder to be a beginner. Her husband had moved up in the world. She had acquired an expensive wardrobe, a very impressive home, and other social symbols of success. And, of course, she was ten years older and felt that she had to live up to an even more intellectual image. Jane had long since lost that open-ended quality of the person who can continue to grow.

Identity transitions require that the person take on the *risk* of fitting into a new niche, a different way, an activity or role or relationship that will make life more meaningful. Listen for a moment to Laura, who, at twenty-seven, was not aware enough of her changing self to realize that she was ready to make an identity transition.

"I have a terrible time—at my office, you know. My boss expects me to do all sorts of little things. So I have to go downstairs, leave the building, and so on. Now, our office is on the fifth floor. But—that's it—I'm afraid to ride in the elevator. I don't know why. But I just get so scared that I'd rather walk. So I go trotting up and down those damn stairs ten times a day, and I get very tired of it! Yeah, I sure do."

But the therapist thought that Laura was further along than she thought she was. He immediately proposed that they go to the nearest elevator. First, they rode up and down a few times, with Laura pushing the buttons. Then they tried it with the light out. Laura immediately flew into his arms, trembling. But after one or two trials, she became more confident and just stood there by herself. Then came the part that she was most afraid of—being caught between floors, in the dark, and not being able to get out. But she pressed the stop button and they were there. A minute later she did this with the light out.

Then the therapist stood outside on the landing while Laura repeated all these steps by herself. She saw him through a window in the door each time she got to the second floor. Finally, he went to his office, while Laura went through these steps several more times all by herself. The entire procedure had taken about fifteen minutes.

Laura rode the elevator in her building from that day on. She need not have been so surprised at the seeming ease with which she had overcome her phobia. She had been becoming generally less fearful for some time. Laura did not realize it yet, but she was getting ready to shed the clinging, helpless, dependent self with which she had functioned in the marriage that she was on the verge of leaving. She was emerging into the adult woman, and the readiness with which she overcame her phobia was but one reflection of the change that was taking place within her.

Those who are insecure fear identity transitions. They are reluctant to take on new roles, while at the same time wanting to. Most of the time they explain their reluctance as maturity and adulthood, saying that they cannot move on to the new levels because of their responsibilities to the old. Actually, they are afraid to risk appearing inadequate. They find support for their attitude in all those people who, like themselves, have given up an exploratory attitude toward life.

They may refuse to engage in exploratory *fumbling* behavior because they are likely to fail at first. Yet, only if their behavior were instinctual could they hope to come by maturity without a fumbling, learning process. Even instinctual behavior, such as sexual activity, requires learning for its proper expression. The way the human animal, as the most highly evolved of all animals, expresses his instincts *involves a great deal of learning.* He may have a powerful sexual instinct, but he must learn how to express it. He does not always learn to do so in the same way. He may fumble a great deal because of this learning factor. His early, fumbling attempts may be regarded as successful in that they pave the way for more precise and effective behavior later on.

If he can accept his fumbling behavior, he will feel free to experiment, to remain open, and so to reshape his identity in a continuing growth process. This is true of any stage of development—walking, talking, social behavior, sexual relating, becoming skilled on the job, or becoming a good marriage partner. Without a willingness to fumble, he cannot develop fully.

The person who has not created enough meaning tends to have a negative outlook on life. No matter what situation he is in, he may project the worst possible outcome. If a difficulty arises in his business, he exaggerates it into a crisis that he feels will surely lead to bankruptcy. If he has problems in his marriage, he may be convinced that they will disrupt the relationship altogether. If the woman he is courting likes to be taken to fancy restaurants, he foresees a spendthrift wife who will want to buy everything in sight. Though his predictions are unrealistic, they become so real to him that he soon reacts to them as *facts.* He worries about the false crises that he himself has created, when what he should be worrying about is his failure to create meaning.

However, actual crises, for which he is unprepared, may arise. He may have to confront an emotional crisis, such as divorce or the death of a loved one. He may suffer loss of position and status, loss of financial security, or a severe accident. Unconsciously, he may have felt that *he* would never have to face such events. As a result, the sudden change may overwhelm him, so that he breaks down. His sense of identity may be shattered. Living includes setbacks, and the person who is realistic must expect to confront them.

People always retain elements of former identities,

even though they change. If these are not absorbed into their current identities, their behavior will deviate from the values and goals to which they would like to adhere. As conflict blocks their capacity to act consistently, they feel a loss of identity. This was especially true of Paula.

Attractive but still single, Paula felt that she was on the verge of a complete breakdown. She was twenty-eight. Her life seemed utterly empty to her. She was incapable of dating. She had dated a great deal at one time but had found it stressful to break off with a number of the men to whom she had become attached. The very thought of starting a new relationship terrified her, for it might end and then she would feel like a failure again. Paula felt almost completely alone in the world, reacting with fear, depression, and loss of hope to the emotional vacuum in which she lived.

That Paula's outgoing, social qualities were blocked may be understood as an identity problem. She was not certain of what she was really like. Actually, she wanted to be someone she was not capable of being. She wanted to be a modern miss, a swinger who could go to bed with a man on short acquaintance and enjoy it. She was drawn to men with money, flashy cars, and smart clothes, men who played it cool and were likely to proposition a girl early in the game.

But Paula's childhood and adolescent training caused her to feel guilty about sexual relations outside marriage. As soon as she became intimate, she had to feel she was in a love situation, one that would end in marriage. Yet because of her insecurity and poor picture of herself, she felt that she could not hold a man's interest for long. This led her to fear that he would surely stray, something she simply could not tolerate. Her fear of infidelity was increased by her general distrust of men. And the type of man that she *could* picture as being faithful seemed stodgy and boring to her. She felt he would make marriage such a drag that it would surely end in divorce, something that she felt she could not survive.

If Paula was ever to come out of her emotional vacuum and relate to a man, it would have to be to one who stood for marriage, fidelity, and children. She might discover that such a man could also do interesting things with her outside the home, that he did not have to be hopelessly boring, and that he might be a better sexual partner than the flashy type of man. Once she could relate closely to him, she would experience the meaning that such a relationship creates. Then she would also find the meaning that would be released from other sources once they were no longer blocked by her emotional vacuum. As things were, Paula's life was empty and painful as a result of her identity confusion.

Chapter 9

Woman Today

The women's liberation movement has brought many identity issues and problems to the fore. It has thrown down a challenge not only to the emerging woman but also to the man.

In his long struggle to broaden his basic rights, the man has been reluctant to extend his gains to the woman. When he won the right to acquire property, he did not acknowledge her equal right to do so. When he demanded the right to vote, it was for himself alone. And when he thought to educate himself, he saw little reason for her to do the same. His identity kept changing as he took these steps to develop himself. Hers also changed, but in directions that resulted in her continued subordination to him.

It was not until the woman struggled for these rights that she won them. Of late, she has been catching up rapidly in privilege and status. No longer is she too passive and dependent to take an active part in situations that call for intellect and judgment. Her present position in business, the professions, politics, and education reflects this. Today she scoffs at household drudgery as the peak of feminine achievement. And all these changes are helping her to overcome the sexual inhibition that has been typical of her.

Yet while she may be receptive to changing values, she may still desire the old. She often looks to the man for guidance even as she revolts against her subordinate role. After all, there have been long generations during which she was kept in the background. *Perhaps she is understood best as being in rapid transition toward equality.* So today she faces the challenge of maturing toward the new levels on which she would like to function.

But it must be said that the man often interferes with her progress. He would show greater maturity were he to prefer a wife who is free to realize her best self. The more advanced she is, the more fulfilling will his relationship with her be. When he broadened his own identity to the neglect of hers, he exchanged the full-blown woman and person that she could have become for one who is too much the dull housekeeper.

The more extreme feminists are impatient with this situation. They want to destroy a system in which the man always comes out on top at the woman's expense. Women are entering various fields more and more, and probably it will not be long before they will gain full recognition in them. In public life, for example, our foreign policy, social institutions, and politics would benefit greatly from the woman's traditional qualities—a concern with peace, child-rearing, and love. These are the core of her older identity, and they can become the core of a newer identity with which she can take her rightful place in society.

How has the domestic role to which so many women object come about? Historically, as wealth grew, service in the homes of the wealthy was more in demand. But while the hired domestic was paid a small wage, the wife's service was taken as an expression of her love. In time, skillful household management became a virtue that was expected of a loving wife and mother, and she became the principal menial in her own home.

This is still true despite the ever-increasing number of educated women. In fact, those who are more educated tend to marry men whose homes are more elaborate due to their higher incomes. As a result, the domestic role has become even more important. Meanwhile, the conflict between the woman's broadening personality and her domestic role has sharpened. The problem is not quite so great for the few who have servants.

Many a wife would earn about as much as the average husband if she were paid the going rates for domestic work. But because she works within the home and does not draw a salary, much of what she does tends to be devaluated and taken for granted. Typically, the man has refused to treat her as an equal with regard to the control of their money. And every woman knows how easy it is for him, because he controls their money, to hold her accountable to him. Until recently, she has gone along with his being the boss. Even when she earns money outside the home, she has tolerated his attitude that what she produces should be under his control, too. This is how it comes about that an irate husband may snarl at his wife, who works both within the home and outside it, "All you ever do is spend my money while I keep working my ass off to make it!" In states that do not have community property laws, the woman's years of work go unpaid if she divorces her husband. Actually, it is as if she has paid for her keep during the years of their marriage through menial work. And, need I add, she has thrown in various fringe benefits that a wife usually offers her husband.

A growing number of women support themselves and compete successfully with men in business and the professions. Often, in their choice of a husband, they are less concerned than women used to be with how much he earns, for they feel that they can rely on themselves. Of course, along with these changes, their feminine identity is changing, too. As a result, some of the traditional distinctions between masculinity and femininity have become blurred. It used to be that major roles were assigned either to the man or the woman. The woman ran the home, and this was feminine. It was up to the man to run the farm or shop, and this was masculine. But the overlap in their activities and roles today confuses the issue.

Each major role calls on the person to carry out certain behaviors. These behaviors are neither masculine nor feminine in and of themselves. They are simply *necessary*. When the woman enters the traditional areas of the man, this does not mean that she is behaving in a masculine way. She is merely doing what needs to be done to carry out that role. The man who washes the dishes because his wife has worked all day outside the home is not being feminine. He is simply being fair! The reasons for thinking of housework as feminine no longer apply when his wife is also at work. He has to adapt his idea of what is masculine and feminine to the changing situation. He is "masculine" in the best sense, *because he is mature*, when he refuses to take advantage of her.

The man who is insecure needs to have the woman remain dependent and inferior if he is to feel adequate. The "advanced" woman does not seem very feminine to him, especially if she reaches the executive or professional level. At that point, she may earn more money than he does. However, while some situations may require her to act forcefully if she is to carry them out well, in others she may be able to use her charming and gracious qualities. In that case, she will appear to be quite feminine even to the insecure man.

Must the woman who wants to become the equal of the man become like him? Must she sacrifice her femininity? Not at all! Equality and sameness are not the same thing. She is already his equal to a greater extent than is ordinarily realized. Her ability to put herself in the other person's shoes, her helping attitude, and her intuition are more effective in many situations than his power, competitiveness, and aggression. If society is to survive in the face of the nuclear threat, her feminine qualities may be the key to the problem. While positions of status and power are still held mostly by men, in a few countries women are already heads of state.

Until recently, the American soldier's readiness to fight bravely for his country was considered masculine. But this is yielding to some extent to the view that it is braver to resist fighting for one's country if the position it has taken is immoral and unfair. This is a far cry from the unquestioning patriotism that has always been typical in masculine identity.

In this writer's opinion, masculinity is also changing in regard to obedience to parental values. The young man may reject the view that it is masculine to become like his father, whom he sees as holding outworn, irrelevant values that do not make for survival. Today's young man may be very concerned with the control of nuclear weaponry, the elimination of war, and the preservation of the environment. He may be more responsive to the needs of the underdog. He is likely to be more aware of the world situation in which he finds himself. He is more inclined to devote himself to some cause that preserves life or that contributes to life as he wishes it to be. Perhaps it is sometimes more appropriate now for the son to instruct the father. Perhaps some of those who are young should serve as models for those who are older.

Amidst these changing views of patriotism, parental values, and the urgency of environmental control, the young man can be confused as to what is masculine. He does not want to be seen as feminine, so he is afraid to exchange his aggressive quality for one of love. Yet his masculine identity is influenced by the new feminine identity, so that he, too, is more actively concerned with the preservation of life.

But this whole trend is still in its infancy. Even though the woman is entering many fields outside the home, her feminine identity is still largely dependent on her personal relationships. Indeed, if she does anything important outside the home, it is seen by many as neglect and, therefore, as unfeminine—as if the home were all she should concern herself with. And masculine identity is still primarily dependent on the man's job and achievement. This is true even though he works, in the first place, to provide a secure setting for his personal life.

Should the man's masculinity be centered more on his personal life? His identity would have more in common with that of the woman if he accented the personal while she moved toward job roles. They would probably get along better. For the past seventy-five years their roles have diverged, hers toward the personal and his toward activities outside the home. This has been a major factor in their becoming less capable of understanding one another. The woman's new status will go a long way toward healing this breach. Now they can share mutual interests and goals as equals. Abraham Lincoln observed that a nation half free and half slave could not survive. Personal relationships also fail under conditions of inequality.

Tradition, rooted in the myths invented by the man to control the woman's sexuality in his own interest, has foisted on her a muted sexuality that inhibits her even when she would be free. But her sexual behavior is changing rapidly today. Though it used to depend on what the man desired of her, now she is being assertive *to get what she wants for herself*. She is demanding sexual equality with the man. Still, as we saw in the case of Paula on pages 96 and 97, she is not always comfortable with her new sexual freedom. In response to the man's suggestion that she sleep over after only brief acquaintance, she may feel shy or eager, inhibited or excited, insulted or flattered.

Of course, the woman who is really liberated refuses to adopt the passive attitude to which the man's response to her is usually keyed. But he may then see her as hard, cold, and demanding, and he stays away from her. In fact, though he desires sexual relations, he may avoid her just because she takes the lead. For one thing, this threatens his feeling that he is in charge of things. For another, the more sexually expressive she appears to be, the greater the threat she represents if he is inhibited.

But if the woman's sexuality is often muted, the man is by no means the sole cause. Her own personality may block its expression. She may be afraid to expose herself to the risk of being rejected. This may lead her toward "safe" relationships in which she cannot possibly become too involved. She may become interested in the married man, in the man who appears at a resort with his fiancee, or in the man who is about to leave for Europe or the opposite coast. Insecure, she contrives what is little more than a facade of response to the man.

She is driven into relationships by her poor picture of herself, which causes her to look for immediate proof that she is desirable. This contributes to her permitting intimacy so quickly. Also, she is afraid that the man may not want to see her again, so she makes it worth his while. But he soon finds that she has mastered the art of "hit and run." Though she showed great interest in him at first, she may drop him before he has a chance to drop her. This is how she may decide to deal with her anxiety about getting involved with him.

It has been pointed out that one of a person's greatest needs is to enjoy a sense of community with others. Most people achieve this only with their own sex. Is it realistic to seek it with the opposite sex, too? Not very, as long as the man and the woman react to each other mostly as sexual beings, not as long as they maneuver, openly or subtly, always in the hope of relating physically. This keys them to one another in an exploitative way. But the more the man sees the woman as a person of worth in a rounded way, the more they will experience community with each other. Incidentally, they will also be better able to sustain the combination of sex and love that they desire because the attractive *non*sexual qualities that they discover in each other will give impetus to their sexual relations.

But can this more mature relationship be achieved through hasty sexual encounters? The current emphasis on living in the here and now is valuable, but it has been put to an immature use. There is nothing in a here and now approach to life that calls for denying the future. The present becomes even more important when it is more than itself alone—when it is also a building block of the future. This emphasis on the here and now has hurt many people today in their personal and sexual relationships. They have tried to find relief from the stresses of life in brief sexual adventures that lack closeness and love. But a relationship that is part of an ongoing involvement takes on a meaning far greater than one entered into just for the moment.

The single woman in her thirties is often concerned about forming an important and lasting relationship. But strangely enough, and often in the name of liberation, her relationships are superficial. She meets someone briefly, looks him over, and if she likes what she sees, she spends a great deal of time with him and becomes intimate. Because she is often a "loner," she is starved for attention and affection. It feels so good not to be alone anymore, and it is so exciting to explore someone and be explored. But this seldom leads to a feeling of security, meaningfulness, and belonging. Nor can she fulfill goals of love, marriage, and children in this way, or combine her sexual and affectional needs in the man. All too often her emancipation is no more than a pose.

To many people sexual intercourse is a symbol of love and acceptance. But the symbol may be empty if intercourse takes place on a first date, when two people are virtual strangers. Their haste suggests desperation and loneliness rather than a basic attraction. Once two such lonely people set up a relationship that presupposes closeness, acceptance, and understanding, they may feel the need to maintain a front with one another. Otherwise they are afraid that they will not be able to retain the prematurely established "interest" of the other. They thus sacrifice being open, real, and truly communicative.

In part, their haste is due to the trouble they have in meeting the opposite sex. The atmosphere of the lectures, discussion groups, and classes that they attend, hoping to meet someone there, appears to them to be cold and unfriendly. It seems as if the only way to meet anybody is to be forward and aggressive. Yet if the man takes the lead, the woman is likely to be wary of him. She is sure that he is interested only in sex. If the woman takes the lead, she may feel that she is inviting the man to make sexual advances. All in all, it is a sensitive situation for many, causing them embarrassment and anxiety.

As modern trends conflict with old the woman fumbles her way toward new patterns of marital interaction. It is not easy for her to catch up with the kind of woman that she hopes to become. But she is deeply dissatisfied with the role she is playing within the home at present, so she is challenging the man more and more openly. In many cases it has become too humiliating for her to continue to try to manipulate him, even subtly, as she often felt she had to do in the past to gain her ends. In manipulating him she cannot gain the feelings of personhood that she desires. Yet, as she expresses herself she sometimes acts immaturely, as if ignoring her responsibilities were the way to emerge as a person.

This has been shown in Henrik Ibsen's play, *A Doll's House*. The reader who is familiar with the play will recall that as far back as 1879 Ibsen tried to create a liberated woman in Nora, the play's leading character. Disillusioned in her husband, with whom she interacted as little more than a compliant child, she abandoned him and their three small children. It did not occur to her to remain in the home and work out their problems. This would surely have been a maturing process for her. Since she had no training for the business world, it may be assumed that coming into her own meant no more than becoming a servant or governess in someone else's home. Ibsen intended his heroine to symbolize certain qualities that the emancipated woman would possess. But the behavior through which he had Nora seek freedom and equality was hardly valid.

Similarly today, certain women's libbers have walked out of their homes altogether. Like Nora, they hope to find their better selves through giving up the roles of mother and wife. True, they are turning away from the *subordinate* ways of carrying out their responsibilities to children and husband. But it is something else to throw aside *the responsibilities themselves*. In doing so they fail to confront the challenge of meeting responsibilities as an equal and as a person of worth. Perhaps turning her back on her marriage is all that the woman can do when her husband believes strongly in the superiority of the man. But many husbands are not so narrow and overbearing. It is hardly likely that the woman will develop herself best through a series of intimate relationships, or, in some cases, through relations with her own sex. Yet, when she does this she may think of herself as being in the forefront of the feminist movement and of progress. Today's liberated woman may well resist conforming to the false value of the man's superiority, but she must be sure that her resistance relfects her growing strength and maturity, not her neurosis and self-centeredness.

On the other hand, even when the woman tries to move responsibly toward equality and maturity in her marriage, she may be thwarted by a domineering husband. Elena had great difficulty subordinating herself to Walter, who was incurably chauvinistic. The demands he made on her reduced her to little more than a domestic, and she resisted them initially. But she felt that she had to maintain the family intact for the sake of her two small children. So she swallowed her pride and put up with Walter's domineering.

Walter was short, but he stood so straight that his carriage was almost military. He had no use for rubber heels, preferring to click his leather heels smartly as he walked. He liked people to know he was around and that he was important. Walter was rather skinny, but he more than made up for his slight frame by the aggressive, dogmatic conviction with which he expressed his opinions. There was one way to do things, one way to think, one way to feel—*his* way. Anyone who disagreed with him was not merely different, but wrong and inferior. Walter was only twenty-seven, but he acted as if he knew it all, even with men twice his age. One can only guess at the insecurity that lay behind his cocky exterior.

Elena, a serious blond girl of twenty-five, had allowed Walter to appropriate her about five years before. She had regretted her decision many times, but they had two lovely little children and she felt trapped. While Walter had come to this country from Europe when he was seventeen, she had arrived much earlier. As a result, she was more thoroughly Americanized than he. And like most American girls, she did not feel that her home should revolve entirely around her husband. But Walter, *General* Walter, as she often thought of him, emphatically did. And he was so firm about it that in order to live with him at all, she had to do as he wished.

Walter insisted that she be responsible for waking his Lordship in the morning. And she had to do so several times before he got up. Breakfast waited on his wish. The whole family adjusted to him when he was ready to use the bathroom. Then Elena would have his clothes laid out for him, and his shoes shined. And when he was ready to leave, incredibly, she had his car warming up for him. He earned $250 a week, but he went to work in the style of a tycoon. Elena's fussing and catering seemed no more than appropriate to Walter, who openly regarded himself as quite a man. But Elena thought he was just an overgrown, bullying infant.

Walter was very insecure because of an unconsciously poor picture of himself. His failure to make his mark in the business world had not helped him either. Nor did his feelings of sexual inadequacy. Elena's yielding to his every whim was essential to his feeling of being a worthwhile and important person.

If the woman is to feel that she is living beyond the level of the supermarket, laundry, and kitchen, or the problems and duties that her children present, she must combine the homemaking role with an important role outside the home. Of course, certain middle-class women of good education have always been able to do this and not violate the needs of either role. But most women are not so self-sufficient. They require the support of others, and they find this in the women's liberation movement. In fact, the movement often does more than merely offer support—it actually needles them into a state of discontent with their roles.

It is probably true that the liberation movement would be much larger if all the women who feel trapped and frustrated at home were able to change their life-styles so that they could follow a career, too. But many of them cannot do this because they have severe identity problems. They have not even been able to carry out the roles of wife, mother, and homemaker to their satisfaction, much less take on a job, too. Still, many of them have to try family life before they can discover that they are not cut out for it. Unfortunately, their husbands are often more wrapped up in their work than in their wives and children. Since these women have only the world of the child with which to fill their emotional needs, their adult identity suffers. They would like a more exciting life-style, too, one filled with more adult interaction. Frustrated in this, they come to feel that marriage enslaves them. As a rule, they have not developed the giving qualities that are so essential in marriage.

Though in her frustration the woman is quick to blame marriage, she must look within herself, too. Actually, marriage can satisfy many of the needs of the person who can flow with it. It offers the woman a sense of "clan" through her own and her partner's relatives. This offsets the indifference of the large city, which otherwise heightens her feeling of being alone. Marriage provides economic security for her and the children. It gives her a stable sexual life. It is a relationship that lasts. And perhaps most important of all, it provides a setting in which to rear children and to develop close ties with them and her husband.

About sixty years ago the woman's activities and goals lay entirely within the home. Her involvement in the family to the exclusion of most other interests did not cause her to have a poor picture of herself, at least not consciously. But today she may feel restless and trapped when she is exposed to the stimulating influence of the liberation movement. It tends to release feelings that many women have had but were unable to express. They not only want a more varied and interesting life, but they want it *now*.

The woman who cannot find satisfaction within marriage often suffers what has come to be known as the "housewife syndrome." She is tired, bored, and discontented. Though she may feel guilty about having such feelings, the thought that her potentials are not being brought out gnaws at her. One study of how the housewife spends her time at home suggests why she has the syndrome. For the period 1920 to 1970, the hours devoted to care of members of the family *decreased* from 9.5 to 8.8 hours a week. Meanwhile, those devoted to preparation of meals, dishwashing, washing, ironing, sewing, and care of the house *increased* from 29 to 40 hours. This took place even with all the advantages of modern appliances! Is it any wonder that the woman develops the housewife's syndrome when she spends so much time in menial, impersonal tasks? Why does she devote so little to the care and training of her children and to personal interaction? It is these that contribute the excitement, joy, and growth involved in family life. If she will expand the mother and wife roles greatly and organize the housekeeping role to minimize the time it consumes, she will have gone a long way toward overcoming the worst effects of the housewife's syndrome. No one will argue with her that many sides of homemaking are sheer drudgery. They drain her ambition and stifle her creative qualities. But there is a great deal that she can do about it. Elaine is a woman who finally took herself in hand after suffering the syndrome in its worst form.

At twenty-eight, Elaine Preston was at her wits end as to how to continue in her home and marriage. She had been married at eighteen, right out of high school. As far back as she could remember, no one in her family had ever gone to college. So Elaine was not a woman who made life at home rewarding through reading, special interests, or a concern with the social and political issues of the day. This would not have been easy to do even if she had been so inclined. Her four boys, ranging in age from two to eight, managed to drain her of every last ounce of energy. She could not afford any help with them, since the Prestons operated on a rather limited income.

There were days when Elaine did not know her own name, days spent in frustration, tears, depression, anger, and pain. She dealt with her frustration by eating constantly. She gained so much weight that she felt very unfeminine. Though she was a strict Protestant, for the first time in her life Elaine could understand how other women might drink, use drugs, or seek excitement outside marriage.

Not that Charles, her husband, did not love her. She felt that he tried hard to help her and understand what she was going through. But it never seemed to be enough, no matter what he did to help. It was almost as if she relied on him to pump some kind of excitement or meaning into her life. But when he went to work and left her with the children, she felt empty and depressed. Some days things reached the point where she thought of ending her life. She had the housewife's syndrome in the worst way.

For a long time Elaine had been feeling that she was just a nobody. She simply had no satisfying sense of identity at all. She felt that she was good for nothing but to prepare lunches, do the laundry, clean the house, shop for groceries, take care of the children, and do a little plain sewing. She felt she was a drudge. She could see no future before her except to slog her way through each miserable day.

It never occurred to Elaine that she was not ready for motherhood, especially for being the mother of four tireless boys. They had arrived within the space of seven short years. Elaine felt that she had become a breeding animal. She was convinced that marriage was a terrible thing. She had no awareness of the immature way she functioned within it. She did not realize that she had had grave emotional problems before she ever got married. Marriage merely brought them out.

She knew that she needed something to save herself from drowning. She was absolutely desperate. She had heard of the women's liberation movement but had always scoffed at it. Yet she was too frightened to just let things go on as they were. She felt completely isolated, almost disconnected from herself, as if she was in the power of everybody else and no longer owned her soul. *Finally, she realized that she had to focus on herself as someone separate from her husband and children.* She decided to join forces with other women in an effort to set up some realistic goals for herself. This gave her a feeling of support. Gradually, she made plans to return to school, with a view to becoming some type of professional person—perhaps possibly even someone who could help other women to find themselves.

The present division of roles within marriage—the woman as homemaker, the man as provider—is rooted in childbearing. It is also an outcome of the industrial revolution. As business and industry developed into large-scale enterprise, the division of labor became much more distinct. The man had to leave the home or farm to work elsewhere, and the woman remained at home with the children. So it is not the man who has forced all the disagreeable household tasks on her, while he lives it up in the outside world. He performs a great amount of dull, trivial work himself, as part of his job. It will surprise no one if the assembly-line worker envies his wife. At least she can pass from diapers to dusting, from dishes to laundry, or from grocery shopping to cooking, without being paced by a production schedule of someone else's making.

The liberationist's view of the man as trying to keep his wife subordinate is probably too severe. Many women, like many men, simply are too immature in the way they go about being married. This was true of Elaine. She did not really want children, at least not four. And once she had them, she never rose to the challenge of what motherhood is really about—the development of their potential through understanding their growth needs and by providing a close and loving relationship. Nor was she independent enough to depend appropriately on her husband, instead depending on him for things that she should have been able to handle by herself.

Marriage tends to call on the woman to belong first to everyone else in the family rather than to herself. But if she is to function well within it, she must be permitted to be a person in her own right, and after that, a wife and mother. Further, she must be able to picture a future that holds a meaningful and satisfying life for her. As things have been, the mother who raised children could look forward only to their growing up and leaving home. If she is to look to the future with hope, she must have her own separate interests and goals. She should have available to her a part-time activity that really challenges her. Then, when her children no longer need her so much, she can expand this activity into a full-time occupation if she wishes.

It is up to society to absorb the woman into its workings in such a way that she can become a complete person. The world outside the home must change the attitudes that prevent her from playing roles for which she is thoroughly qualified. The women's liberation movement might do well to bring pressure to bear on industry and the government to introduce the half-time work day for mothers of school-age children.

When the mother of young children holds a full-time job, as an increasing number do, she may naturally feel that it is unfair to expect her to carry out the homemaking role all by herself. The man who expects her to do so usually feels that it is not masculine to share the homemaking role with her. Or, he may simply be exploiting her.

A 1973 study of suicide by professional men and women throws some light on the problems of the career woman. Female psychologists commit suicide three times as often as other women. (The male psychologist does so somewhat less than other males.) Female medical doctors also commit suicide three times as often as women in general. Female chemists have a high suicide rate, too, and even nursing is somewhat above average.

In explaining their findings, the researchers suggest that those women who have emotional problems to begin with may be drawn to these professions. They are urgently seeking some meaning in life. But to maintain their position and responsibilities they often must give up marriage and a family. (Only one third of the female psychologists who committed suicide were married.) Otherwise, they are in great conflict as they try to carry out both roles.

The researchers then go on to make what to me is their most interesting suggestion: "A sense of role conflict may not be limited to married women. For women brought up with a traditional role-orientation (marriage), achievement of a career *without concomitant development of a family* may also carry a psychological penalty." Where women's liberation pictures the frustrated housewife as longing for some type of career outside the home, here the career woman is pictured as longing, perhaps unconsciously, for a family.

If part-time employment were fostered nationally, the woman could combine marriage and a career in a manner that would do justice to both. At present, when she tries to combine both roles she usually has to carry them out *on a full-time basis*. But the man, who regularly combines a career with marriage, does not involve himself in the home too fully. His career takes most of his time and energy. It is hardly fair or realistic to expect the woman to carry out both roles fully *as they are presently set up*. As has been suggested earlier, the family would be better off if the man did not emphasize his career role at the expense of his role as husband and father. This would make it easier for his wife to combine both roles in better balance. The work week is steadily getting shorter, so that the man should be able to devote increasing time to the home.

While the present form of marriage may not have come about as a means of subordinating and exploiting the woman, it lends itself to such ends today. It is up to the man to open his eyes, his ears, and his heart if he wants to really understand how the woman feels about marriage. If he is going to be fair (and if he is not, the woman will force him to be), he will have to spend time sharing the parental and homemaking roles. Those who can afford it will no doubt have a servant to help them. One thing we can be sure of is that as the woman continues to develop herself, marriage will have to be changed. It can remain an effective form of relationship only if society is flexible enough to do this.

Chapter 10

Existential Living

What are the people like who think and live existentially? They are more than a little skeptical that science and technology hold the key to the good life. They are somewhat disillusioned about man's ethical nature. And well they may be after two world wars, the constant jockeying for power spheres in the cold war, the increase in crime, the fouling of the environment, and the harsh, unconcerned attitudes toward the welfare of others that are so prevalent.

In the search for meaning a person may be drawn to a number of ideas found in existential thought. He can come to terms with everyday existence by seeking meaning *within himself*. He defines reality largely as what is within him. His is not a conformist reality, for he believes strongly in his own standards, style of life, goals, and sense of personal worth. As these guide his thoughts and behavior, they create meaning for him. He believes strongly in his own values, too. He tends to emphasize them rather than material things, realizing that he can never keep anything for very long, not even his life. Nevertheless, because his values and style of life are culture-bound, the meaning that he creates is sifted through and bears the imprint of the people and institutions that surround him.

Keenly aware of the empty, even absurd, quality of so much of life, the existential person combats the resulting anxiety and apathy by striving to tap and develop the potentials within himself. In existentialism's emphasis on *freedom of choice*, combined with responsibility for whatever that choice may be, he discovers that, as his own man, he has something significant to say about the course of his life. Facing the demand of modern society for specialized expertise, he combines the achievement of long-range goals such as becoming a doctor, businessman, or university professor, with existentialism's insistence on living in the here and now. Aware of his thoughts and feelings, he penetrates to the core of what he is involved in doing at any given point in time. As has already been pointed out, he experiences the present as even more meaningful precisely when it builds toward the future in addition to being immediately gratifying. Indeed, certain types of situations absolutely require that they be linked to the future or they lose their power to be gratifying in the present. Wilma found herself in such a situation.

Wilma, thirty-four, broke her engagement to Sam, thirty-five, three years ago. But she still sees him periodically, usually on an intimate basis. At their last meeting she and Sam went out with another couple. They had a very enjoyable evening, after which Wilma spent the night with Sam.

The next day, Sunday (a day that allowed her to become aware of her feelings), after she had had breakfast with Sam and returned to her own apartment, Wilma suddenly felt empty and depressed. She wondered why the night before seemed to be so completely in the past. She did not realize that it was because it was not linked to an outcome in marriage, home, and children on which she had her heart set. She was hurting because in some things the here and now is not enough. It must be linked to the future if it is to create meaning.

Everyone needs a major area of activity if he or she is to create meaning in life. For many men their work satisfies this need. It provides them with an activity in which they can use their abilities. It gives them a sense of purpose as they move toward their goals. They feel competent and important when others depend on them. The activity that occupies the central place in the lives of the majority of women is the rearing of children and the marital relationship.

Every activity is made up of certain essential, inherent elements. When the person engages in the activity for the sake of these elements, he is being existential. For example, being a tennis player is about physique, general athletic ability, and court strategy. It satisfies the person's needs to keep fit, develop grace and balance, and belong to a group. But he may use it to meet members of the opposite sex, to pass time that hangs heavily on his hands, to make contacts for his insurance business, to prove that he is still physically virile, or to escape the dullness of his business or his life at home. The more he focuses on these, the less he plays for the sake of the game itself. As a result, he fails to function existentially.

The person may seem to be existential because he is absorbed in his work and activities and is surrounded by people. But sometimes the situation in which he finds himself may be such that he cannot function existentially and must make a decision to change it. Despite the motions he goes through, he may not really be *in* his work. He may be *distant* from his children, *at odds* with his wife, or *fail to value in and of themselves* the activities that lead toward his goals. Under such conditions the absurdity and aloneness of life press in on him. Henry Adams, a good example, was very unhappy as a result of functioning in this way.

Because of his liberal social and political views, Henry Adams, forty, an associate professor of sociology at a rather conservative university, was at odds with the clique of professors that ran the department. They refused to advance him to full professor, and he could not get an increase in salary. Meanwhile, the high rate of inflation had reduced the buying power of his salary to the point that his family had to tighten its belt.

Henry had branched off into a school of thought that was original with him and a handful of professors scattered around various universities in the country. His work seemed rather strange to his colleagues and probably threatened them somewhat. They spoke negatively of his journal articles, especially when he came up for a salary review.

There had been one bright spot in Henry's life at the university—the students. He had always enjoyed the interaction with them. But recently he had been given some elementary courses to teach that were very heavily attended, so that few student contacts were possible. Henry found himself teaching in a bored, mechanical way.

His ability to do research and write articles seemed to dry up. He felt frustrated and guilty about this. And as the other professors continued to scoff, he came to feel that his ideas were not worth much. At this point he was working only to earn his salary. He felt lonely and isolated in the classroom and in the department. While his salary was essential, it alone could not make up for what he was missing.

Henry finally turned his back on the university. He took a position with a government agency. Here, instead of being an outcast, he was in charge of a number of men. And they accorded him the respect that he deserved. Almost at once he felt better. The fatigue and depression that had weighed him down at the university disappeared. He put in long, hard-working days, yet felt fresh and alive. He produced research and articles that were well received. His satisfaction spilled over into his family life so that when he was at home he was really there with his wife and children. He was living existentially again. His salary, a secondary consideration now, was soon considerably higher than it had been at the university.

People who live existentially undertake activity not only for its own sake but also for the goal to which it contributes. Their concern with the future does not necessarily lack existential quality. So long as goals are realistic and directly related to current activity, they are existential. Thus, a medical student may be interested in studying anatomy and neurology for themselves. He or she does not have his eye on the status that being a doctor will give him, the swank office that he will have, and the money that he will make. Because he is interested in his studies for themselves, he will be absorbed in the practice of medicine later on, not just in the money he will make. That his studies are linked to the future does not violate their existential quality. Some of the person's most important activities require planning and foresight, and often this is when they are most meaningful—going through a complex program of schooling, progressing in one's job over the years, consistently saving money for a home, or bringing up children who are prepared to take their places in the world. But this is not to suggest that behavior must be linked to a future goal to be existential. The office worker who basks in the sun over the weekend just because he or she enjoys it is being existential, too.

It makes sense to react anxiously under certain circumstances, and such anxiety may be thought of as natural or existential. Will the person recover fully from an accident or illness? Will he adjust to the loss of a loved one? Will he or a loved one be killed or wounded in the war? What will he do with his life now that he has failed to accomplish what he set out to do? It is appropriate for a person to show anxiety in such situations. But if he remains anxious and upset for a long time after an unfortunate event, this may be his way of justifying his failure to carry out his customary roles and responsibilities. In that case, his anxiety no longer arises from the original event, as he continues to pretend, but from areas of his personality with which he cannot deal. He cannot live this anxiety through as long as he continues to pretend that it arises from the immediate situation. It is not surprising that he remains depressed for such a long time.

In order to keep existential anxiety from becoming neurotic anxiety, *the person must accept the former*. His anxiety becomes neurotic because he tries to feel better about himself through some type of maneuver. He may avoid facing a stressful situation or lay the blame for his own inadequacy on others. These maneuvers or games or ways of making believe change existential into neurotic anxiety. Existential anxiety is part of *being*, whatever one may be, while neurotic anxiety points to a fear of being openly whatever one is.

The person may value what is threatening and painful to him, even though it arouses his anxiety, because he has lived it. He values it because it has been part of his life. He risks expressing his *whole* being when he can accept possible pain. But if, for example, in response to an expression of intense feeling *by someone important to him*, he jokes or becomes witty and clever because he cannot confront the other's feelings and tries to deny their existence by joking, he is failing to accept the existential anxiety that is a part of the situation. If he did not do this, then, even though he would be openly stressed, he could live his anxiety through by coping with it in one way or another. Failing to do this, he fails to be existential, and he is alone. He has isolated himself from what was most meaningful between him and someone important to him.

The person might like to set the boundaries within which his life can take place safely. But life cannot be made safe for him. It is better for him to learn to "roll with the punches" than to hope to stay in the ring without ever being hit. It is mature for him to take all reasonable precautions against painful events, but if he refuses to accept them and the anxiety that goes with them, his anxiety, now neurotic, will be multiplied many times. Many of the situations that he avoids are the very ones that make life worthwhile. Thus, he or she may relate in a distant way to those to whom he should be closest, afraid of being hurt if he becomes too involved with them. But he denies himself love, warmth, and understanding, and in so doing he reduces himself to a state of relative nonbeing. While nonbeing in a final sense means death, it can also mean unimportance, meaninglessness, or aloneness. The person who is reduced to nonbeing becomes anxious. His anxiety is neurotic rather than existential because it arises from his distortion of relationships rather than from his natural reaction to the hazards of relationships. Joan is a good example of a woman who could not make the decision that would free her of the defensive, inauthentic relationship, saturated with fear, in which she was living.

When Joan, forty-three, had married Harry, fifty-five, she had been drawn to him because he seemed like a strong figure of a man. She felt she could respect and admire him. But they had not been married long before she realized that he was so insecure that he had to control everything. Their sexual relations deteriorated so that they felt self-conscious with each other.

This was a second marriage for Joan. After her first, she had developed to some extent as an independent woman. But in order to live with Harry and not quarrel constantly, she had to go back to being as passive and compliant as she had been in her first marriage. She found this very difficult to do. She supported herself and her two children as a schoolteacher but felt that she needed the financial security that Harry represented. So she tried to communicate openly with him about their problems. But Harry blocked any type of discussion that implied he was less than perfect. He insisted that she adapt to him completely. Joan debated whether to leave him. Meanwhile, she kept trying to appear contented while inwardly seething.

Because of her own fear of the future, Joan was not living existentially with Harry. She found her day by day life humiliating. Coming home to Harry at the end of each school day had become something that she dreaded. Weekends, when they were together so much more of the time, had become pure torture. But she could not admit failure in marriage a second time. She tried to be contented, but she could not become absorbed in her life with Harry. There were too many times when she pictured a future that would be happier because it would not include him. She was certainly not living existentially.

Underneath Joan's surface fears lay her unconscious fear of involvement in a close relationship. Harry certainly provided all the distance she needed before she could feel safe. She continued to cling to her frustrating marriage because, though she wanted closeness very much, she did not dare risk it.

Many people still turn to one of the oldest and most universal methods of dealing with their existential anxiety— resignation, faith, and religion. They hand their anxiety over to God, so to speak, relying on Him to assure them of salvation and a way out of life's troubles. They find security in life through love of God, thinking of Him as their guardian Father. And surely it is meaningful, for those who can so believe, that an all-powerful, all-knowing Father is looking after them.

While people always have some choice, their freedom to choose is reduced by a number of influences over which they have little or no control. It is limited by unconscious sides of their personalities and by their training and life experience. The extent of their knowledge gives direction to their choices. Their heredity does so to some extent, too. Accident and illness influence it. In the end, death denies them any choice whatsoever. Each of these fixes the limits of their choice so that their behavior cannot be as free as they might wish.

A person may find it difficult to make an important decision, not only because of the existential anxiety but also because of the responsibility he or she would have to assume. Insecure and fearful, he cannot stand another blow to his picture of himself should he choose unwisely, so he may maneuver to have someone else decide for him. Then, should he be unhappy with the outcome, he can blame the other person. Meanwhile, unconsciously, he holds onto a picture of himself as capable of choosing more wisely and maturely. But in doing so he evades the challenges that would contribute to his development. Sometimes he is convinced that he has no choice but to act in a certain way. Actually, he is unwilling to accept other choices. To do so he might have to give up something, risk facing up to someone, or show himself in an unfavorable light. He might have to change, perhaps to the extent of making an identity transition. A different decision or choice might call on him to change his lifestyle, give greater recognition to the needs and rights of other members of his family or friends, or spend money without which he is too insecure. Or he might have to relinquish the emotional support of someone who is very important in his life. She may no longer meet his needs, but he clings to her for fear of finding himself without any emotional life at all.

So a woman often acts as if she has only one choice, when actually she may have a number of others that would be more beneficial to her. Once she understands why she has not even considered these other possibilities, she can see how feasible they really are—provided she is prepared to change. Lisa in the following example showed this in the way she maneuvered unconsciously to remain uninvolved with her husband.

Thirty and married, Lisa was best friends with Helen, who was single. Over her husband's violent objections, Lisa felt that she had no choice but to talk to Helen about the most intimate matters concerning her marriage. Her husband, Harry, resented not only his loss of privacy but since Lisa adopted the ideas and attitudes that Helen drilled into her head, felt that he was practically living and coping with both of them. Finally, he put his foot down and insisted that Lisa choose between him and Helen. Forced to the wall, Lisa chose Harry. It was understood that she was to break off all contact with Helen.

But Harry had not reckoned with Helen. *She* absolutely refused to accept Harry's terms. She kept insisting that she had a right to talk to Lisa all she wanted, reminding Harry that she had known Lisa long before he had. But Harry was adamant.

It soon leaked back to Harry that Lisa was in frequent touch with Helen. When he challenged her on this, it turned out that she felt helpless to stop Helen. Though she had refused to talk, even hanging the telephone up when Helen called, Helen would call back again and again. When Lisa took the receiver off the hook, Helen wrote her a letter, or sent a telegram, or sent a message via a common friend. Worst of all for Lisa to contend with, Helen would come knocking at her door. Helen insisted that in her heart Lisa really wanted to continue their friendship but was forced by Harry to pretend that she did not. This was more or less true, so that in the face of Helen's persecution Lisa felt that she had no choice but to talk with her.

Lisa was not aware that she was emphasizing Helen's persistence too much. She could choose not only to hang up when Helen telephoned but also to throw away her letters unopened, return the telegrams unread, not permit a common friend to transmit a message, and absolutely refuse to open the door to her. But before she could take these steps, she would have to understand that she chose to act as she did because she used Helen as a buffer between Harry and herself. She kept their relationship a cold and distant one. Only after she understood this, and provided that she would choose to relate more closely with Harry from then on, could she be firm enough to say "no" to Helen. What made it so difficult for her to do this was the undercurrent of homosexual awareness between Helen and herself.

Chapter 11

Sexual Arousal and Climax

Orgasm in a woman is a sensitive indicator of the existential quality of sexual relations; that is, to what extent a woman is involved for sex itself not for other, nonsexual needs. About 11 percent of American women never have had this natural response to arousal, while an additional 14 percent have seldom experienced it. This usually defines the woman as being frigid. But frigidity is best understood in terms of *all* inadequacy of sexual response, and in the man as well as the woman.

Because the woman's sexual zones are more or less internal, she must be fully caught up in the act, that is, function existentially, if she is to have orgasm. That the man's sex organ protrudes results in stimulation even when he is not entirely "with it." In masturbation, the woman can have orgasm repeatedly because in stimulating herself she is focused on pleasurable sensation. So it cannot be said that she is *sexually* frigid when she fails to have orgasm in intercourse. Her frigidity is psychological in origin, because she is unconsciously afraid of being hurt and cannot give herself up to the sexual act. She has learned to withhold herself so that she will not need the other person too much. This is how she probably interacted with her parents, and she transfers it to her adult relationships. She does not realize that, since she relates distantly to the man, things are bound to turn out poorly. Then, having kept him at arm's length and after having lost him, often to another woman, she concludes that she has been right all along in believing that men are not to be trusted or depended on. This experience reinforces her fear of serious involvement. Of course, she has nothing to fear in masturbation, when she relies on herself.

The woman who fails to have orgasm is often determined to achieve it. But her very determination violates the existential nature of sex. Orgasm is the outcome of arousal, not of determination. Many of her other motives violate the existential nature of sex, too. She may have intercourse so that she can regard herself as a normal, expressive woman. She may be trying to give her husband the feeling that he is thrilling her. Or, she may hope to hold his interest so that he will not turn to other women. She may be trying to relieve her anxiety over difficulties in their relationship, taking sex to be an act of love. When she puts sex to these nonsexual uses, she is not likely to have orgasm. There is even less chance of doing so when she goes along with her partner's desire for intercourse, though she herself is not so inclined.

Another influence that contributes to her frigidity is her guilt and inhibition. At first, she may be carried along by the excitement of the early stages of the relationship. But after a while her response diminishes steadily and remains inhibited no matter how much she tries to react intensely. Nor is this surprising, for while certain cultural values train her to respond to the opposite sex, other cultural values block this response. The media of entertainment and advertising create a widespread sexual atmosphere. A great many physical and social activities—swimming, tennis, dancing—encourage her to be sexual, too. But at the same time, many traditional, religious, and moral influences inhibit her. And her sexual expressiveness is often discouraged during the first twenty years of her life, when her drive is very intense. This may prevent her from acting freely later on.

However, if her motives in having intercourse are existential, she may feel adequate as a lover and is likely to be esteemed by the man. She may depend on intercourse to express her tender feelings with intensity. She affirms her femininity, as does he his masculinity. They both gain reassurance of their continuing love. This reassurance is likely to be more important to the woman than to the man if she is to lose herself in the act and have orgasm.

The man seldom fails to have orgasm. His frigidity appears less openly. While he seems to be responsive to the woman, his sexual behavior may lack passion. He is self-contained and aloof. When he is not really "with it" he may cough, clear his throat, or sneeze, reactions that never occur when he is really caught up in sex.

The withdrawn quality of a man's sexual behavior dulls the woman's arousal. She is aware that he merely uses her as an object to satisfy himself. His frigidity, like hers, appears in the way he wards off what he fears most—a warm, close relationship. This fear makes him hostile to the woman when she tries to involve him and colors his sexual behavior, too. He may tolerate only the most limited foreplay, and he may either lose his erection or satisfy himself long before she has an orgasm. Yet, on a conscious level, this undercurrent of hostility is masked as he plays at being in love by initiating intercourse.

In fact, he may initiate intercourse *excessively*. What marks it as excessive is not its frequency, though this is likely to be well above average, but that he fails to lose himself in the act. He is so frustrated within himself and with his life that he tries to drown his unhappiness in sex. This is hardly existential. In addition, he needs the feelings of dominance and masculinity that he gets. Afraid to lose his partner, he may try to satisfy her so completely that she will not look elsewhere. He may quiet nagging doubts of homosexuality by proving that it is the woman he wants. Through it all he may be sincerely convinced that he is "making love."

The frigid man is likely to go in for outlets that are even more distant than his style of intercourse. He may fantasize intensely about a woman who hardly knows of his existence. He may spend hours looking at nude pictures, or he may peep cautiously through windows to see what he can see. Though such behavior is only indirectly sexual at best, he becomes very aroused. Situations that lack the reality of physical contact, being safe, allow him to give free rein to his imagination. But when he has actual relations with a woman, his excitement vanishes. He *uses* her, but he does not allow himself to *need* her.

Ordinarily a quick, intense reaction implies youth, health, and vitality. Many men are proud of their ability to ejaculate quickly and vigorously. But many men who are more highly educated tend to delay orgasm as long as possible. They use various techniques that lessen their arousal. They assume that this makes it easier for the woman to have orgasm, convinced that she is not as sexual as they are. These men don't understand, however, that they sacrifice the existential quality of sex when they manipulate their own arousal. Not only are they themselves not "with it," but neither are they very stimulating to the woman. They thus defeat their purpose. Were they to act spontaneously and passionately, their excitement would arouse their partners.

The man may inhibit the woman by asking about her orgasm. He may do this in a subtle way, but it destroys the existential quality of their relations. She reacts by making orgasm her goal, instead of letting arousal take over. Yet it is most unlikely that she will ever reach a climax this way. Alexander Lowen, a psychiatrist who has written insightfully on sex, has described this in his book, *Love and Orgasm*:

> To govern the timing of the ejaculation by the response of the woman destroys the natural flow of feel-

ing that alone guarantees mutual satisfaction. This point cannot be stressed too strongly. Inhibiting the buildup of the excitation for the sake of the woman limits the possibility of mutual satisfaction, whereas the opposite enhances that possibility.

The woman's orgasm is often important to the man's picture of himself as someone who is exciting to be with. Nor is she herself certain that she is truly a fulfilled woman until she enjoys orgasm regularly. So man and woman both focus on bringing her orgasm about, not realizing that they are bound to fail because they are not being existential.

Sometimes such lengthy sexual play is substituted for orgasm that it is doubtful whether the partners are functioning in an existential manner. Susan is a good example of this.

Susan had been seeing Jim, a married man, for seven years. They engaged in very long foreplay, forty-five to sixty minutes. Susan thought this was wonderful, though she seldom had orgasm. But by the time she was thirty, recognizing that it was getting late for her to marry and raise a family, she broke off with Jim.

Bill, her next boyfriend, was quite different from Jim. He would enter her after a few minutes of foreplay and soon ejaculate. Susan never had orgasm. She felt cheated out of the lengthy stimulation that Jim had gone in for. Her therapist defended Bill's sexual style. He suggested that Bill was acting normally, but that she was acting like a very inhibited woman. When Susan got over her huff with the therapist, she proceeded to modify her attitude. Within two weeks she reported, in utter amazement, that she was joining Bill in orgasm after just a few minutes of foreplay. She indicated that he was sensual with her in general, not just prior to intercourse. But she decided that Bill was not suitable as a husband for her, and she dropped him.

Susan's next boyfriend, Sam, was a handsome man. She valued his looks highly, almost above everything else. She became engaged to him after only three months. But once again she had a sexual problem. This time, however, things were turned around. Sam was somewhat inhibited sexually and seldom took the lead. So far as Susan was concerned, he let things drag on and on. The very techniques that only six months before she had found so exciting in Jim now frustrated her with Sam. She found herself "going dead" on him, he took so long to get to what was now her main satisfaction, orgasm. That she did not go back to lengthy foreplay suggests that it had been carried on *in place of natural, speedy arousal and orgasm.*

I have broadened the term *frigidity* to include self-contained, withdrawn, hostile sexual behavior. Now the phrase *sexual intercourse* requires some attention. The prefix, *inter*, meaning between, should be taken literally. Intercourse takes place between two people, *being an act of mutual stimulation and response.* It is not an act in which one person engages by himself while in the presence of the other. When the man "masturbates" in the woman, he mainly stimulates himself. When the woman becomes aroused by passively allowing the man to stimulate her, then she, too, is centered chiefly on herself. *Inter*course takes place when their arousal is achieved by what they do to and for each other, as well as themselves. Of course, the mutuality that is typical of satisfying, existential intercourse must be present long before the couple have actual relations. It must saturate the foreplay. But the person who is afraid of displeasing or losing his partner, and concentrates on pleasing him in the foreplay and in intercourse, is not having *inter*course, because he is centered on his own security instead of sexual arousal. So now foreplay, like frigidity and intercourse, needs to be discussed.

Foreplay is usually taken to be the intensified mutual stimulation that takes place prior to the man's penetration of the woman. This stimulation may range from a half hour to two minutes, depending on how slow to arousal the particular woman is supposed to be. But there is more to foreplay than this. It goes on for hours between two partners. Their eyes meet, their hands touch, and each is aware that the other is sexually attuned. It is an *atmosphere* between them. They know they are going to have intercourse at some point, and they are warm, open, and responsive to one another. The woman may feel herself to be lubricated, while the man may occasionally become erect. This is foreplay in its best sense.

Of course, most people stimulate each other much more intensely just before intercourse. But some couples stimulate each other *only then*. Their sexual behavior does not arise naturally between them, but seems suddenly to come from nowhere. Very often it leads to intercourse in which one of the partners is hardly aroused, so that he or she is likely to feel used. The woman, for example, may not even be lubricated, while the muscle at the entry to the vagina may be so constricted that the man can enter her only with great difficulty. If she is at all frigid, she certainly has little opportunity to become less so under such conditions.

Repeated relations with the same person tend to become dull. Newness, exploration, and conquest, which do so much to heighten arousal, are no longer present. At this stage the person who cannot combine love with his sexual relations will find it difficult to sustain them. Unfortunately, all too often his feelings of love have worn out. Yet it is only when love is blended with sex that each partner becomes more or less *uniquely* capable of satisfying the sexual needs of the other. Otherwise, many a physically and sexually attractive person can gratify each partner as much or more.

This suggests that when two people who love each other have intercourse, some of their *non*sexual interaction has its outcome in sexual arousal. Admiration of how a child is handled on a particular occasion may be expressed through sex. So can support and help in solving a perplexing problem. A conversation in which each partner feels deeply understood is likely to lead to sexual relations, too. In general, feelings of gratitude, appreciation, and warmth are readily expressed through sex.

Intercourse demands more of the man than of the woman. He must have a firm erection, enter her, and sustain his erection long enough to complete the act. His self-esteem is keyed to a picture of himself as at least a competent, if not a passionate, lover. If he fails to sustain his erection long enough, he may feel negative about future intercourse because his virility has been called into question. Many men are sensitive about their virility when the woman fails to reach a climax.

But the man who loses his erection may be at least as aroused as his partner. However, she may be quite critical of him, for her failure to become fully aroused is not as obvious as his. In fact, it may be her passivity that causes his problem to begin with. Once the novelty of exploring her has worn off, his arousal is dulled in the tedious effort to get her to respond. But he tends to accept the blame because she *seems* to be able to perform her part. Actually, she has only to allow herself to be penetrated, and she will appear to be more or less adequate. She thus does not become anxious and question her capacity for arousal whereas a man might very well question his virility. Nor can she see any reason he should not find her satisfying. Interestingly, often she herself enjoys sex even though she does not achieve orgasm.

When the woman is stimulated by firm, rhythmic, consistent touch, she is as quick as the man to reach a climax. But she can hardly do so when he delays, talks, and interrupts himself. Real differences between the two in the capacity for arousal must depend on differences in anatomy and physiology; yet no such differences are known. The man appears to be more aroused by a variety of memories, sights, thoughts, and situations. This may be partially why he engages in more masturbation, premarital intercourse, homosexuality, and extramarital relations. But a large number of women are very responsive sexually. Undoubtedly they represent the woman's potential for arousal better than those who are inhibited.

The average woman, who is married at twenty-one, reaches her peak of arousal about nine years later. She is so inhibited that it takes her all this time to overcome her fears enough to have orgasm. Her partner is often most eager for intercourse just when she is inhibited and reluctant. By the time she can express herself more fully at thirty, his drive has been declining, especially since he usually is somewhat older than she. Her drive, though still less than his, remains about the same until she reaches forty-five. So the gap between them gradually narrows.

Though the woman may not overcome her inhibition until she is about thirty, she continues to free herself for many years thereafter. Then, when she turns forty and as a rule has less to do to care for her family, her sexual drive may become more important. The approaching change of life, with its decline of sexual attractiveness and capacity for arousal stimulates her to greater awareness of her sexual nature. She may face it with a sense of impending loss and become temporarily more interested in sex. And she no longer fears pregnancy. These influences contribute to maintaining her frequency of orgasm in the period preceding the menopause.

Two types of sensation are typical of the woman's orgasm. Sometimes clitoral sensation is most prominent, as when she masturbates or when the clitoris is fully stimulated in intercourse. At other times she may be most aware of sensation arising from vaginal muscle in spasm, either in masturbation or in intercourse, especially when orgasm results from the pressure of the penis against the walls of the vagina thus discharging the nerves that are more deeply imbedded. Thus her orgasm may be thought of as differing types of sensation arising at different sites. The clitoris is comparable to the penis. Its stimulation is as essential to the woman's orgasm as stimulation of the penis is to that of the man. There is some evidence that women in whom the clitoris has been removed cannot have orgasm. But orgasm can occur without vaginal stimulation. Many medical doctors report that about three-fourths of all women have never had, as they experienced it, a vaginal orgasm.

Whether a woman finds orgasm something to be enjoyed or to feel guilty about depends partly on where she feels it takes place. Its location is quite controversial. The view that it is vaginal has been the traditional one. The ancient Jewish codes, designed to foster reproduction, found only vaginal stimulation permissible. The Christian codes, derived from them, have continued this teaching. Though our society is not as concerned with reproduction, our sexual values are still influenced by this tradition. Many people feel guilty if they violate it. For them, the location of the woman's orgasm is a moral matter.

Some writers have called the "maturity" of clitoral orgasm into question. They point out that it is the clitoris that is stimulated in masturbation, which is thought to be immature because the person is not in a sexual relationship with another. They argue that homosexual relations, centered on the clitoris and vaginal lips, are abnormal. And they point out that petting to climax focuses on the clitoris. None of these has its outcome in offspring or encourages the person to take on social roles. These critics feel that because the vagina (really the uterus) is linked to reproduction, it has special virtue. They regard those who ignore what might be called the vaginal values—marriage, children, home—as immature and as having failed to achieve complete womanhood.

Yet the vagina has relatively few nerve endings, so that it is not very stimulable. The chief sites stimulated in intercourse seem to be the clitoris and the vaginal lips. These are precisely the sites that are stimulated in women who masturbate, relate homosexually, or pet to climax. It is true that these types of stimulation are often immature. The wife may avoid her partner by masturbating; the homosexual may be afraid of the opposite sex. And petting to climax may replace vaginal entry. But the clitoris remains the chief organ of orgasm, no matter what parts of the body are stimulated to begin with. There is something naive about the "morality" of various tissue responses. The woman who locates her orgasm in the clitoris, no matter what the type of stimulation, need never feel guilty about it.

Perhaps the man who regards the vagina as the site of orgasm does so because then he becomes essential to the woman's satisfaction. Over time, many women have come to believe that orgasm should take place in the vagina. Freud played his part in perpetuating this notion. It is certainly true that the vagina and the clitoris have a common wall, so that sensation *arising initially* in the vagina may be hard to distinguish from sensation in the clitoris. This often gives rise to the impression that orgasm is vaginal.

Part Three

Professional Help

Chapter 12

Psychotherapy

Most people try to find help when they feel upset or depressed. They are likely to talk with the neighbor next door, a close friend, a relative, a parent, an attorney, a medical doctor, or a religious adviser. But though these people are eager to help, without realizing it, they may express their own problems instead of helping the person in terms of *his* or *her* needs.

The psychotherapist does not bring his own problems into the situation. He can prevent this because he has insight into them, and he is trained to be objective. Clients reveal their problems more openly to him than to their own marriage partner or most intimate friends. In fact, clients are likely to look at their personality patterns more deeply and honestly with a therapist than in the privacy of their own thoughts. They take courage from the therapist's acceptance of their immature qualities and thus can accept them more fully themselves instead of denying them.

The therapist helps the client realize whether what he or she expects of relationships is realistic. He helps bring to light clients' obscure motivations, hidden fears, conflicting desires, and inadequate sexual patterns. As a result, clients can make constructive changes in their life-styles. They make better contact with the realities of their lives. They stop yielding part of themselves by overconforming to the wishes of others. They recognize their maneuvers to avoid the anxieties of life. They learn to use knowledge of their past to improve their present behavior. Therapy points the way in which they can risk a new response, so that they are not bogged down again and again the same old way. They rid themselves of symptoms and patterns that upset them. Usually they develop a more accurate picture of themselves, of their strengths and weaknesses. Often they become more expressive of their emotions. And they are very likely to become more creative in their everyday life.

Many people are accustomed to thinking only of the more severe emotional disorders as calling for professional attention. Even though they may find their life-styles dull, they tend to think of themselves as normal because they do not present a clear-cut neurotic picture. But others, even though they are functioning fairly well, find therapy helpful in developing the maturity to live more fully. These are the people who get the most out of therapy. They succeed in doing so because they have greater stress tolerance, and this enables them to examine their limitations more candidly. In addition, they are secure enough to risk changing their behavior, which is the goal of therapy. Unfortunately, the greater the client's problems, the less benefit he usually derives. He is too resistant, defensive, and inflexible to risk making changes. A comparison can be drawn between a physically disabled person who can barely perform beneficial exercises and makes little progress, and someone who is merely "out of shape" and can benefit by doing similar exercises vigorously.

A sample dialogue of what goes on between a therapist and client can give only an incomplete picture of that particular type of therapy. For the most part, these sample sessions are real, though some of them have been created to represent real situations. Such a brief dialogue, together with a summary of the method, can at least introduce the reader to what a specific approach has to offer. So, after a brief explanation of the features common to most therapeutic methods, I will discuss several types of therapy, pointing out the aspects that make each unique. In doing so, while it is expedient to refer to the therapist as "he," it should be pointed out that a considerable number of therapists are women.

All therapists try to establish warm and friendly relationships with their clients, that are built on mutual respect. They listen as sympathetically and as sensitively as they can. They usually react to their attitudes and behavior as openly as possible. Most psychotherapists, except psychoanalysts, try to reveal themselves as people.

The client may expect help in overcoming his or her immediate stress and frustration. Many therapists meet this need, but others have goals that take longer to achieve and involve basic changes in the client's personality. To accomplish this, they ask a variety of questions that not only yield background material but also get the client to think about important areas of his or her life and behavior. In addition, questioning by the therapist avoids long silences and passivity on the client's part.

The therapist is always *acceptant* of the client just as he or she is; he does not judge. This creates an atmosphere that is free of threat. Clients must feel secure if they are to explore themselves and if their potential for growth is to assert itself. The therapist particularly accepts the client's negative qualities. The client cannot find such complete acceptance from anybody else, and this helps bring about the special relationship between them that enables him or her to grow.

All psychotherapeutic approaches try to help clients make constructive changes in their behavior. These changes represent new learning and, as such, contribute to their growth and maturity. To facilitate change, the therapist brings out the distortions of behavior that prevent clients from living more existentially. He employs various techniques to help clients become keenly aware of their feelings. He encourages clients to have a favorable picture of themselves in every valid way.

This enables clients to change more readily. The therapist's ability to place himself in the clients' shoes and share their experience helps clients overcome the sense of isolation that has contributed to their inability to deal with difficulties in new ways. The therapist is supportive and reassuring, letting his clients know that they have a strong, caring ally who will stand by them as they risk changing.

Psychoanalytic Therapy

Even though the client determines what he will talk about during therapy, the psychoanalytic therapist helps him bring many unconscious wishes, attitudes, and ideas to conscious levels by obligating the client to say everything he thinks of and by analyzing his dreams and slips of the tongue. He interprets any resistance that the client puts up, bringing out the unconscious material in this way. His goals for the client are maturity, the capacity to live up to one's potential, and spontaneity through changing the personality.

The psychoanalyst is concerned with feelings, but he does not focus on them. He does not give advice or criticize. But he does ask many questions, gaining detailed insight to the history of the client's personality. He encourages him to relive his emotional conflicts so that he can discharge the tension they arouse. He adopts a parental attitude and in this way brings out reactions the client used to have to important figures in his childhood. These reactions are distorted because the client projects onto the therapist qualities possessed by people who were influential in the client's earlier life. The therapist then interprets these distorted reactions, *always being careful to reveal nothing about himself, thereby remaining a very neutral figure to the client*. This practice of encouraging and interpreting the client's irrational, transferred reactions to him is the foundation of psychoanalytic technique.

Many psychoanalytic therapists make interpretations only when the client is prepared for them. Therapists of other persuasions employ interpretation as a stimulus rather than a summation in order to get the client to see the connection between his or her behavior and its result in a much shorter time. This technique may cut into the rapport between therapist and client, for the client may be upset by a "premature" interpretation. But if the client feels that he or she is progressing, rapport with the therapist will remain adequate.

It is only on the surface that the relationship between the therapist and client is a permissive one. Actually, the analyst is quite authoritarian. His attitude is that of a teacher-father. His interpretations are usually made with an air of finality. He gives the client the feeling that he is dependent on the therapist's interpretations to understand his own behavior and statements. He encourages a parent-child atmosphere through the use of the couch and an emphasis on early childhood. And while the therapist demands that the client say everything that occurs to him, he himself remains a blank screen.

The psychoanalyst also explores a client's dreams to reveal personality, believing that they point *symbolically* to feelings and how one deals with them. The client's stress may be pictured more clearly in dreams than in anything that he or she is capable of saying, and it may be relieved through dreaming. Occurring when the activities of the day no longer occupy the mind, some dreams point to desires that a client may not be prepared to face. They reveal the conflicts that prevent one from expressing drives. Many dreams of assertion against authority figures are of this type.

A man of thirty-two in his sixth month of psychoanalysis.

Client: I would say my father was quite strict with me. He expected me to live up to his ideas of a man, what a real man should be. I know I would never have dared . . . .

Let me drop this for now. Something else is bothering me. It keeps coming into my mind, so I might as well tell you. Last time, at the end of the hour, when we were standing at the door a moment, talking, I was very uncomfortable. And I have noticed the same thing at other times, too, when I have stood alongside you, or facing you.

Therapist: Why do you suppose that is?

Client: I am not sure, but I keep noticing how much taller I am. Why that should make me uneasy—well, more than that, actually—quite tense—I don't know. (*Pause.*) I remember, when I was a boy, I used to admire how tall my father was, and my brothers, too. Then when I started to grow, I shot up and became the tallest one in the family.

Therapist: That ended your being the baby of the family?

Client: Yes, well, I was the tallest, but maybe I was still the baby for a while. (*Pause.*) I'm not sure, but I think while I felt great about being so tall, in a way I didn't like it either. You know, when a boy looks that big you expect him to act like a man. (*He is expressing dependency longings.*)

Therapist: You weren't sure you could do that yet.

Client: As a matter of fact, my father let me know many times that I still wasn't meeting his standards just because I had grown tall. Sometimes, in a way, I'm still not sure even today. But I kept on competing with him and with my brothers, and I guess I have never gotten over feeling that I'm still doing it.

Therapist: And it makes you feel—uneasy?

Client: I feel as if they want to cut me down to size, the way they used to. My brothers, too. Yes, they all did it. Maybe I imagine some of it today, but I really think they do have that attitude toward me, in a way. You could say I've gone ahead of both my brothers (the client is a successful engineer), and, of course, I'm much more educated than my father. It's like a constant struggle that goes on, only no one says anything about it. We all just do it but never mention it.

Therapist: And now you're taller than I am, too. (*Preparing client for an interpretation.*)

Client: Hmmmm? Yes, I am taller than—is that why I am uncomfortable standing next to you?

Therapist: I think so.

Client: But why? I am taller than lots of people, but it doesn't bother me.

Therapist: You're not competing with them. (*Interpretation.*)

Client: I am competing with you?

Therapist: Yes. Just as you always have with your father and older brothers.

Client: (*Pause.*) I am thinking of an idea I sometimes have—about you—and it's the same as I have often had about my father—if I stood up to you as an equal, as a man, you might squash me; you wouldn't admit I'm your equal. Of course, I'm not, in many ways, yet I am a person like everybody else. (*Distorted reaction to the therapist as if he were his father.*)

Therapist: So when you stand up alongside me and are taller, it's as if you are asserting you have surpassed me. And because you react to me in certain ways as if I were your father, you feel I won't like it. Then you become anxious, expecting me to try to squash you in some way. (*Interpreting the client's distorted feelings.*)

Client: Yes, that feels right.

Therapist: You know, whenever you say anything in your own favor, are you aware in what a mild, unassertive way you say it? And then in the next sentence or two you take it back, or most of it. (*Working through the client's distorted perception of the therapist.*)

Client: I didn't realize that. Maybe that's why I'm always so tense when my boss takes me to lunch. Even on the golf course, where I'm a much better player than he is, I'm still tense with him. And with some of the other executives, too. (*Pause.*) If I act like an equal, they may cut me down. Yes, I think that *is* it. I guess when I talk myself down, I'm more comfortable because they won't know how competitive I really am, how much I want to show I'm as big as they are. (*Pause.*) Are they all like my father—to me, I mean? (*Gaining insight.*)

Therapist: In a way, yes, they are. I'm not your father, the person. But I am someone you think you should make the grade with, what might be called an authority figure, like your boss. And just as you handle your need to equal your father and brothers in a strongly competitive way, you do the same with us. And as you fear being cut down with them, you feel the same with us. So you assert yourself, then feel tense, become afraid, and try to appear modest and unassuming. Pretty much the way you used to do and still do to some extent with your father and brothers. (*Continuing to work through the client's irrational perceptions.*)

Client: Uh-huh. And when I react to you as you really are, not as I think you are when I confuse you with my father, I'll feel better?

Therapist: Yes. You'll be living more with reality, not an unconscious distortion of it. That's always better. If I could make a comparison with your own work—you cannot solve an engineering problem very well when you have only part of the data; well, the less accurately you perceive me, my feelings, my motives, my attitudes, the less you are in touch with the real data about me. So, the more poorly you interact with me.

Client: Mmmmm. Yes.

Interpersonal Therapy

Unlike the psychoanalyst, the interpersonal therapist holds that an open and honest relationship is curative. The client's distorted reactions to the therapist provide direct data on his interactive style, and these are analyzed. As the client comes to understand what his behavioral patterns are, he can begin changing them. His anxiety is identified and its origins traced. Its role in his overall functioning is made clear, as is the way he handles it. But the interpersonal therapist's chief concern with anxiety is to discover how it operates in the interaction between himself and the client. The client's history is also important. He develops an accurate picture of himself and a sense of personal identity by tracing it. The history also helps therapist and client to formulate jointly the goals of therapy, deciding what the client can and cannot change.

A *twenty-seven-year-old divorced woman in the fifth month of interpersonal therapy.*

Client: I've been very upset for the last few days.
Therapist: Uh-huh. Because you broke off with George? (*Focusing on her anxiety.*)
Client: Yes. I finally did as you told me.
Therapist: Oh?
Client: Didn't you want me to? Didn't you suggest I do that?
Therapist: Not at all. It was entirely your own idea.
Client: Well! (*She fidgets like a child.*) I thought you told me to.
Therapist: I don't recall ever *telling* you to do anything. (*Corrects the distortion in which she sees him as a father instructing his child.*)
Client: But I wish you would. I wish you would help me *more*—more directly, I mean, tell me what to do.
Therapist: Uh-huh. Jane, tell me, do you notice anything about the way you are dressed today?
Client: (*Coyly.*) You notice what I wear.
Therapist: (*Ignoring her seductive quality.*) Just when you are asking me to be like a papa who tells his little girl what to do?
Client: Am I your little girl? But you *do* notice.
Therapist: Of course, I do, especially when there's such a dramatic change. You sit with crossed legs like a little girl. Even the way you talk, like a child asking me what to do, as if you are helpless, all alone in the big world, asking papa to guide you and protect you. (*Analyzing the distortion in the way she is relating to him.*)
Client: (*Still seductive.*) You're becoming impatient with me.
Therapist: (*Still ignoring her.*) You know perfectly well

what to do about fellows like George. Time isn't for-
ever, you know. You're a Jew, yet you get involved
with an orthodox Catholic. And before that, you got all
excited about Jack—married, and out here only for a
brief visit. (*Analyzing her defensive patterns.*)

Client: Are you jealous of them, doctor?

Therapist: Jane, you know I think you are an extremely
attractive woman, but. . . .(*Presenting himself as a responsive human being.*)

Client: (*Breaking in.*) That's the first time you have ever
said so.

Therapist: Well, I'm not here to be interested in you as a
man to a woman. Jane, you know very well what I am
saying—that you start things with men with whom you
know you can never really develop a relationship. You
get sexually entangled with them, but you are not
involved.

Client: (*Sincerely.*) I could get involved with you.

Therapist: Not really. No more than with them. You know
it can't go anywhere with me either—any more than it
ever could with your father.

Client: My father?!

Therapist: You had all sorts of personal ideas about your father; you know that. And they upset you, naturally. So
you carried on a nice intellectual relationship with him.
He being a doctor, and his cultural interests—you could
do that easily. (*Pointing out her tendency to ignore her
feelings, especially when they arouse anxiety.*) You've
tried over and over to convert our sessions into friendly,
chatty, social talks—psychological theory, sociology,
the way therapy works—all very intellectual. (*Exposing
her distortion of the actual nature of their relationship.*)
That's how you *usually* deal with the anxiety your sexual and emotional interest causes you. (*Tracing the
origin of her anxiety.*) Today is different, I admit.
You've been more open and direct. You fluctuate that
way. Don't you remember, when you first began to
come, how frustrated you were with me because I

wouldn't sit here and chat socially with you?

Client: I wanted you to like me—to appreciate that I am—well, quite intelligent myself.

Therapist: You know I like you. In another kind of situation I would have found you very interesting.

Client: Interesting?

Therapist: All right, attractive.

Client: You are not afraid to say it?

Therapist: Of course not. It's not a thing that shouldn't be said. Especially when we're trying to be completely open with one another. Otherwise, how can we be open with ourselves? But I'm your therapist—suppose I were your neighbor and you were married—it's just not in the situation.

Client: Then I wish you weren't my therapist.

Therapist: Well, sometimes you do try pretty hard to switch me into your boyfriend.

Client: Oh, rarely. I've never been as open about it as today.

Therapist: That's true. Most of the time you've been defensive about it.

Client: How do you mean?

Therapist: Oh, you usually deny your personal interest by being provocative. (*Pointing to her refusal to confront her actual feelings.*)

Client: Is that denying it?

Therapist: The extent to which you do it, and the times at which you do it, yes. In the back of your mind you always know I can't be interested in you as a woman. But you keep presenting yourself as one so I can ignore you, even get irritated at the way you subtly keep on trying. That's how you defend yourself against getting involved with anybody, by antagonizing them with inappropriate interest. At the same time you can think of yourself as a woman who wants to love and be loved. (*Analyzing how she handles anxiety.*) You see, Jane, you're an expert at picking impossible situations in which to present yourself. That's your way of making sure that you'll always be warded off. (*Exposing her maneuver more fully.*)

Client: (*Dully.*) Oh, I'm a dilly, all right.

Therapist: Jane, wouldn't you say that most of the time there's a current of tension between us? (*Insisting on an open relationship.*)

Client: Uh-huh. Yes, there is.

Therapist: That's because of your constant maneuvering to feel like a woman, to get involved, yet not get involved. Jane, why don't we finally accept the situation between us. You have developed a sexual interest in me, just as you did in your father and other men, too. So—no more maneuvers. It puts you under tension— but live with it, honestly, openly. Once you give up these false stop-and-go games, you can develop sincere situations in which your feelings can be returned. That's frightening, I know, but it is the only way you can move toward the long-range goals we've discussed. (*Outlining the goal of involvement.*)

Client: If only I weren't so afraid of that.

Therapist: Yes, but you want it, too.

Client: I always have, underneath.

Adlerian Therapy

The Adlerian therapist feels that the client's past, present, and future are influential in any choice he or she makes as to how to behave in a given situation. Feelings of inferiority also influence the choice. Instead of simply approaching others, one tries to enhance one's self to be more acceptable to them. A person has a great need to express belongingness.

The Adlerian therapist emphasizes treatment of the whole person—in the setting of family, social circle, physical self, personality, and goals. He is concerned with goals *because they influence the client's current functioning just as surely as the past does.* (This approach uses a different emphasis from the psychoanalytic, which stresses the past.) The nature of the client's goals throws light on what he or she is like. The therapist helps the client understand whatever may be unrealistic about his goals. The client need not have a conscious understanding of his motives unless his behavior fails to advance him toward his goals. *So the unconscious in general is not studied.*

Early experiences of a client's life are important to the Adlerian therapist. He takes control of the interview and asks many questions about them. He believes that clients remember only those experiences that fit their present purposes and goals. As goals change, memories change, too. Early memories of the childhood family reveal the client's "basic mistakes." These are the false beliefs about one's self, others, and the nature of life that developed in childhood.

The therapist holds that children do not remain dependent because they are small and weak. Continued dependence is a form of dominance over parents. But as dominance is returned to the parents, the child gradually gives up the dependence and becomes more mature. Sadly, the child's dominance has never given him the feeling of being loved.

The therapist is not afraid to become openly angry with clients. This shows the clients how their behavior would be received in the outside world. It reassures them that the therapist feels that they can tolerate an angry reaction. It allows them to see the therapist as a fellow human being.

Having learned the client's life-style, the therapist analyzes values, concepts, and interaction. He analyzes the client's symptoms, exposing what the client would do *if he or she were able to.* This reveals the purpose of the symptoms, that is, how they defend the client, lessen one's anxiety, or enhance one. When the client grasps how he creates his own problems, he realizes how he can make himself well. The responsibility to do so rests squarely on the individual. The therapist does not try in any direct way to change a client's values, goals, or behavioral patterns, or to remove his symptoms.

A woman of twenty-six in her fifth month of
  Adlerian therapy.

Client: This fellow I went out with on Saturday—he's very handsome. A nice guy, too. We had a good time talking and laughing together. But *aggressive*! Wow! He sure came on like gangbusters!

Therapist: That's an odd combination of qualities, a really nice guy, coming on like gangbusters. (*Taking the lead and preparing to analyze her interactive style.*)

Client: Yeah. As we were driving home I thought about what he would do—saying good-night, that jazz. But I didn't expect anything like what he did.

Therapist: Oh?

Client: He kept insisting we go up to my apartment—he wanted us to—go all the way. (*Vehemently.*) This was our first date! Anyway, I would never go to bed with any guy unless we were married.

Therapist: When you say he kept insisting—what got him started on that?

Client: Oh, we were kissing and—getting kind of worked up.

Therapist: Who started that?

Client: He did. (*Pause.*) I suppose he might say I did. (*Hints at her own responsibility.*)

Therapist: How come?

Client: Oh, when he parked the car I opened my purse to get some gum. I was going to offer him a piece, too, if he wanted it. But then I had only one. So I put it in my mouth—uh, halfway—and let him know he could have the other half if he wanted it. He thought I meant . . .well, he went for the gum and grabbed me with it. Whew! Can he kiss!

Therapist: (*With resignation.*) Then one thing led to another.

Client: It sure did. But I think he could have shown more respect for me—thinking I would. . . .A nice guy like that. At the end I was really angry with him.

Therapist: (*Lightly.*) Perhaps he didn't realize you weren't eighteen yet. (*Challenging her to take responsibility.*)

Client: Hmmmm? What? (*Therapist waits, smiling; her eyes* *drop.*) You think I'm responsible for what happened.

Therapist: (*Seriously.*) You had both been enjoying yourselves together all evening. You invited him to start necking with you. You're not a child, Sue. What did you expect?

Client: (*Pause.*) I suppose I should have known what might happen.

Therapist: *Might* happen?

Client: Are you saying I wanted it to happen, I made it happen?

Therapist: Of course. Sue, this is the fourth or fifth incident of this type you have described. About one a month. You keep playing innocent, but. . . .(*Interpretation.*)

Client: (*Exasperated.*) But I didn't want him to take me upstairs, to make love to me!

Therapist: Well, let's say that you wouldn't allow it to happen. But how can he tell until he tries?

Client: Hmmmmm. (*Pause.*) I suppose it is up to a woman to control what happens. You think I've been unfair to him.

Therapist: More important, unfair to yourself. (*Focusing on how she plays games with herself.*)

Client: Uhhh, I don't give anyone a chance to get near me?

Therapist: You give him the big come-on and lead him to expect you'll go all the way. But you aren't prepared to do that. You're just trying to make sure that he'll call you again. And you do get a lot out of the necking. So you throw yourself at him, then slap him down hard when it's time to come across. (*Analyzing how she creates her own problems.*)

Client: You can be pretty brutal at times.

Therapist: Well, Sue, somewhere along the line you're going to see through your act. The innocent victim of the aggressive male! You're controlling him every step of the way. So there's not much point in complaining. Whatever happens, it's what you want to happen. (*Insisting she take responsibility for what she chooses to do.*)

Modified Analytic Therapy

There are many kinds of analytic therapy. In the modified analytic approach, described here, the therapist offers strong support as he manipulates the environment for the client's benefit. He emphasizes the client's intense reliving of thoughts and feelings. He points out the goals he thinks the client should pursue. He takes into account the client's age, duration of problems, flexibility, desire for recovery, confidence in the therapist, and insight into problems. His directive attitude brings out a dependent quality in the client. This is considered to be all right for mild neuroses in which the goal is to help the client adapt to life more comfortably with the personality the client has already developed.

The use of support in modified analytic therapy often involves control of the client's environment. The therapist suggests that he or she take certain risks or abstain from certain behavior. In order to tailor his suggestion to the client's capacities, he evaluates the client's level of anxiety, skill, and intelligence. If the client is disorganized, the therapist may make certain necessary decisions for the client. Once the client has an ally, he or she has a better chance to build up resources, lessen symptoms, and adapt more flexibly.

A *married woman of twenty-eight in her twelfth month of modified analytic therapy.*

Client: (*Smiling.*) Well, I have some news for you today.

Therapist: Oh? About what?

Client: (*Still smiling.*) Uh, my husband and me. (*Pause.*) I've agreed to his getting a divorce.

Therapist: I see. (*Their eyes meet, while she continues to smile.*) Joan, why are you smiling? All this must be very painful for you. (*Stimulating a forthright venting of her feelings in a supportive way and encouraging her to act openly as she feels.*)

Client: (*Breaks down in uncontrollable weeping.*) I should have known better than to hide my feelings from you.

Therapist: It's better to let them out.

Client: I know, I know. You know how I feel inside.

Therapist: What made you finally decide on this step?

Client: I can't go on this way anymore. Cliff is a baby, a big, weak baby. I don't dare depend on him. Not because he wouldn't try to see me through anything that came up—but he wouldn't have the strength, the maturity. Cliff is a son to me, not a husband. And it's time mother and son were separated. Maybe that way he can become a man and I a woman. Together, neither of us is what we should be.

Therapist: Uh-huh.

Client: All my life I've been afraid to let myself depend on anybody. Oh, it started way back, when my mother practically drank herself to death after my father left us. (*Bitterly.*) I learned real early in life not to trust anyone. And now—here I am.

Therapist: Where are you now?

Client: Well. I realize *I* picked Cliff. Not to depend upon him, but because I *couldn't* depend upon him. Still, I can't go on like that. That much I've learned this past year.

Therapist: Oh?

Client: I learned that through you—that I can depend on a man. The week I was in the hospital [she had attempted suicide]—afterward, I felt closer to you than I've ever felt to anyone. You were there, every day.

Cliff—he had to leave town for his company, that great job of his. . . .For the first time I found somebody who didn't let me down. (*Strong supportive relationship.*) Now—well, I can't go back to living without needing someone badly. I don't need Cliff, he needs me. I don't want to play it safe anymore. Maybe I'll be safer that way. You understand that.

Therapist: I certainly do. (*Strong support.*)

Client: I know it won't be easy. In a way, I hate to separate. I'm afraid. But in a way I look forward to it, too, wondering what's out there. And I'm afraid to stay as I am and shrivel up. (*Insight clear enough to lead to behavioral change.*)

Interactional Therapy

In short-term therapy, the goals of interactional therapy are limited. It aims to relieve symptoms. Long-standing depressions are seldom relieved in short-term therapy. But disorders such as bed-wetting, difficulty in falling asleep, overeating, nail-biting, and smoking do respond to a short-term approach.

The client discovers either that he can carry out the therapist's suggestions or that he cannot. If he cannot, he can no longer ignore this fact. He also recognizes how he relates to the therapist—does he trust him enough to carry out the advice? The therapist may advise him to do just what he cannot even discuss. He also helps him to carry out the advice by assisting in writing a letter, giving him necessary articles, or having him make a telephone call from the office while he is there to offer support. When the therapist is so forceful, he must question the client carefully to be sure the client knows just what to expect.

Many clients run out of things to say and need help to continue talking. Each client has different resources for keeping in motion. The therapist lets him take the lead as long as he can carry the ball. When he is unable to any longer, the therapist questions him so that he will not flounder too long. He may ask where he lived at a certain age, where he lived after that, and so on. The framework may be the schools the client attended or the girls he knew. The client may be able to recall a great deal in this way. His recital may be very emotional, especially if the therapist occasionally asks how he felt about a particular situation. Interactional therapy thus has much in common with "crisis" therapy, in which the therapist may take an active part in helping the client overcome a difficult situation that has arisen suddenly. The interactional therapist must take matters into his own hands to a great extent, for, in the setting of a public clinic in which he often works, he has only six to twelve sessions in which to help the client.

After several sessions of interactional therapy,
a man who just turned twenty-six.

Client: Well, she's done it again. Guess what my mother sent me for my birthday.

Therapist: What?

Client: The same thing as last year, and the year before, and the year before that—a muffler. I have a whole drawer full of mufflers. Boy, my mother is really something. She probably buys six at a time, and then sends me one each year. Look at all the time and trouble she saves shopping. Maybe she even gets a discount—volume buying—or maybe there was a sale. I suppose I shouldn't expect anything else. It's so much trouble to go out each year and buy me a real present.

Therapist: Have you ever let her know you still have the other mufflers? Or that you would like something else? (*Suggesting direct action.*)

Client: No, what good would it do? It doesn't matter enough to her to put herself out the least bit.

Therapist: It would be interesting to see what she'd do if she knew you wanted something else.

Client: I don't think it's up to me to send her a diagram.

Therapist: That's not a bad idea after all. Send her a diagram. I think you ought to return the muffler and ask her to exchange it for something you can use, something suitable for California weather. She's still thinking in terms of Idaho. And let her know that you still have the other mufflers. How about it?

Client: If you say so, but I don't think it'll do any good.

Therapist: Well, I'd certainly like to see you do that. Then we'd know where we stand. (*Firmly intervening and asking for client's trust.*)

Client: All right. I'll set it up for her to slap me down again. No use coming to you if I don't listen to your advice.

Therapist: You have little enough relationship with your mother as it is, and it's a shame to let a five-dollar item interfere with what's left of it.

Four Therapy Sessions Later.

Therapist: By the way, you mentioned last week that you hadn't returned the muffler to your mother. Have you had a chance to do it yet? (*Testing client's confidence in him and insisting on direct action to find out whether he is right about his mother.*)

Client: I suppose I've had lots of opportunities, but I haven't done it, if that's what you mean. I really don't think I should return it. It's only four or five dollars, and it's not worth making her feel I am criticizing her.

Therapist: Bill, would returning it necessarily have to be a criticism?

Client: It sure would! Boy, I'd *like* to send it back, just to let her know she isn't *that* perfect herself. See how she'd like *that*!

Therapist: I wonder why you haven't sent it then.

Client: Well, I. . .I don't know. I want to. But—Jesus, I don't know!

Therapist: You're convinced she would feel criticized if you did?

Client: Boy, oh boy, would she! Yeah, she'd feel criticized all right. And she'd be right.

Therapist: And feeling criticized, she would become very angry?

Client: (*Fidgeting.*) She'd be furious with me. (*Pause.*) That's for sure, she'd be furious.

Therapist: And that's what you're afraid of. (*Interpreting underlying feeling.*)

Client: No! I'm not afraid of her! Not anymore. I'm not a kid at home anymore, dependent on her!

Therapist: Then why is it so hard for you to do something that you feel would amount to criticizing her? (*Insisting on action becomes a forceful interpretation.*)

Client: Nobody wants to criticize if it isn't over something worthwhile. (*Pause.*) You really think I'm afraid of her?

Therapist: I do. Otherwise I think you'd send it back and ask for something else. Bill, imagine this for a moment—you're going right home from here so you can wrap it and mail it to her. Do you think you could?

Client: (*Pause.*) No, I guess not. (*Desperately.*) I don't want to get her angry.

Therapist: The thought of it upsets you.

Client: Yes, it does, it really does. Damn it, you must be right.

Therapist: Talking against her siphons off some of your anger. But it doesn't help you to stand up to her. For that you have to *do* something. And, you know, then you'd find out whether she's as angry *at you as you seem to be at her.* Bill, your own anger might make you misjudge her feelings toward you. Even the idea that she just doesn't care. (*Urging that he check on how he sees his mother.*)

Client: Mmmmmm. And what about you. I mean, are you angry at me for not mailing it?

Therapist: No. (*Bypassing the client's reaction to him as a parental figure.*) I think we've found out something— that you're still afraid of her. Now, by testing, we can see whether there's as much basis for your fear and anger as you seem to feel there is. Maybe we can move now on your relationship with her. (*The therapist's request for action has led to the acceptance of his interpretation.*)

Eclectic Therapy

The eclectic therapist uses certain parts of various approaches, combining them into an organized system of his own. He emphasizes what he thinks is most valuable to a particular client at any given stage of therapy. The more experienced he is, the more leadership he takes in the form of questions, advice, interpretations, or manipulation of the client's affairs. He interacts as a real person with real feelings, avoiding the "blank screen" of the psychoanalyst. The client can not only be open and spontaneous, but even hostile, and be certain that the relationship will continue. He or she will reexamine his own reactions when they do not agree with the therapist's because he thinks of him as someone who is mature. If the therapist expresses a negative opinion about certain behavior, this may be more reassuring to the client than complete approval, for he does not approve of everything about himself. As long as he feels he has the therapist's respect and esteem, he does not require complete approval. For example, if the therapist goes into the client's history to clarify his present behavior and the client uses this procedure to feel sorry for himself, the therapist points out that he has merely developed another defense against changing.

The client's goals are examined in relation to how well his life-style lends itself to achieving them. His unconscious is made conscious so that he will understand more than only a part of his behavior. The therapist may ask him to say whatever comes into his mind and may also interpret his dreams. The client's immature ways of maneuvering are exposed. He learns to make a sharp distinction between anxiety that is inappropriate and anxiety that is a natural part of many situations. But none of these techniques is aimed at moving the client toward some fixed goal. The eclectic therapist does not routinely seek historical material, manipulate the client's environment, get him to express his sex drive, or encourage him to enter into relationships. Any one or all of these may be sought for a specific client.

A woman of thirty in her fourth week of eclectic therapy.

Client: I must tell you I've been sleeping very badly for the past few nights.

Therapist: Oh? Why is that? Any idea? (*Offering her responsibility for direction of the session.*)

Client: I don't know. I've stayed on my diet (*she is short and stout*). Not that I deserve any credit for that—it's just the hypnosis working. Actually, for the first time in my life I don't have to fight it. I'm perfectly content on the diet. But, of course, I haven't lost a pound yet, and it's been a month now.

Therapist: Well, you've just resumed your thyroid medication. (*Suggesting resistance.*) When you went on the diet you discontinued the medication even though you have used it for years to help control your weight.

Client: Yes, but I don't think that will make any difference. It never has.

Therapist: Hmmmmmm. Don't you think there's some meaning in the fact that you discontinued it a few days before your first session with me?

Client: No. Unless it's unconscious. (*She had been through analysis several years before.*)

Therapist: Well, think of it this way. You are very unhappy with your figure. Not only would you like to get married, but in your profession [publishing executive] appearance and socializing are important. You've been reducing for the last sixteen years—and it's never worked out. Coming here was a do-or-die attempt— right?

Client: Yes.

Therapist: So, after arranging your first appointment with me, you immediately go off the thyroid you'd been taking for years. Now that seems odd to me. (*Suggesting unconscious motive.*)

Client: You make it sound as if I don't want to reduce.

Therapist: I think in a way you don't. (*Pointing to conflicting feelings.*)

Client: But why?

Therapist: Well, maybe not that you're afraid to reduce, but afraid of what it might lead to. You are very unsure of yourself. To reduce—get new clothes—really present yourself—is to take a chance. What if you do all that and still don't find anyone? Then you could no longer tell yourself you *are* charming and interesting, even though you're stout and you never go anywhere. Much as you want to reduce, you're afraid to take the test. (*Interpretation.*)

Client: I hope I haven't missed anything you said, but as you were talking I remembered that since going on the diet I have been buying the wrong cola drinks. I thought I was getting the no-calorie type but happened to notice only yesterday that they're just loaded with sugar. They must have changed the label. Or else I'm doing more things to fight myself than I realize.

Therapist: Yes, I think that fits. You know, it might seem as if you are working toward a simple goal—losing weight—but actually it involves a great deal more, doesn't it. The whole picture of your physical self, your relations with men, your job, your mood level—have you been waking up as depressed as before? (*Supportive and probing.*)

Client: Yes. I just don't want to get up in the morning. Uhhh, I was feeling all right until Tuesday—no, Monday—then Tuesday I had a letter from my sister that she's definitely coming out next week.

Therapist: And you've been depressed and sleeping poorly since?

Client: Yes, it's gotten worse again. I can't tell you how I dread her coming. Well, I've told you that before.

Therapist: She has a trim, neat figure and you're convinced she'll despise you. (*Encouraging emotional reliving of these feelings.*)

Client: I *know* that in her heart she does. Last year when she was out here—I'm ashamed to tell you this—you know I told you how I cross the street or go around the block so I don't meet certain people because I can't stand to have them see me so stout—well, last year, for the ten days my sister was with me, I was constantly on edge, standing this way and that—I didn't dare let her see me in profile. I know she would have been terribly disgusted.

Therapist: You seem to feel that very strongly. (*Reflecting feelings.*)

Client: I really don't know what to do, but I don't want her to come. I just don't want her to see me this way. In fact (*Covering her face in shame.*) I wrote her a letter today—forbidding her to discuss my weight when she comes, the way she lectured me last year. I would rather she didn't come if she's going to do that again!

Therapist: You mentioned before that you were especially sensitive if she saw you in profile. Why was that? (*Probing for a symbolic association.*)

Client: Isn't it obvious? That way my weight shows up the worst.

Therapist: Mmmmm, no, not necessarily. For you to maneuver around not to be seen in profile—why?

Client: Oh, I can't stand to be seen that way. Never could. Especially by my older sister.

Therapist: What does being seen in profile mean to you? Do you associate it with anything?

Client: I just feel she would be enormously disgusted with me, terribly, terribly critical. Oh, my God! (*A frightened pause.*) I suppose I must tell you this. When I was eighteen I had an illegitimate child.

Therapist: You? Oh. (*He had expected only a symbolic association between excess weight and pregnancy.*)

Client: My mother never knew. Oh, the deception that called for! I insisted on going to an out-of-town college. Some friends helped me. My mother never did find out, and when I had the child I gave it out for adoption. My sister always said mother would kill herself if she found out; she made me feel responsible for trying to kill my mother. You know, my mother's sister and her daughter had both committed suicide. So I was constantly watching how I stood and dressed and acted. Of course, my sister was watching me like a hawk every minute, constantly making me feel I was taking mother's life in my hands by what I'd done.

Therapist: No wonder you became so sensitive about being seen in profile.

Client: Yes, it must be that.

Therapist: Being stout and paunchy is sort of like being pregnant, unconsciously, and makes you feel guilty all over again. But it may not mean that to your sister. To other people, including your sister, excess weight is excess weight, nothing else. (*Supportive and breaking associative links.*)

Client: (*Relieved.*) Mmmmm, yes. Maybe so.

Nondirective Therapy

The nondirective therapist feels that the client will progress simply as a consequence of being in relationship with him. His techniques are derived from this basic idea. The intensity of his feeling never exceeds the client's. He never praises the client because praise is a form of evaluation, which suggests the right to blame, too. Rather than deal with behavior that the client resists changing, the therapist *focuses on feelings*. Occasionally, he says more clearly what is unclear in the way the client expresses it. Convinced that the client has an innate need to grow, he supplies a relationship that is favorable to maturing. He does not become emotionally involved with the client. Though he imagines himself in the client's shoes, he is not depressed by the client's despondency, frightened by her fear, or upset by her anger. He offers the client the deepest understanding and acceptance. But any hint of seeking to influence her or make her over in the therapist's image destroys the relationship he tries to provide. He does not direct the client's attention toward any particular channels. He accepts the client's statements as they are given and by repeating them offers her an opportunity to hear and react to her own thoughts and feelings. He summarizes some of the client's ideas. He avoids asking questions, giving advice, offering criticism, or interpreting. He gives the client responsibility for the conduct of the interview from the beginning.

From an early nondirective interview of a young woman in distress.

Client: My mother always made me feel I was my father's favorite. Not that I had any special privileges. In fact, they were both strict with me.

Therapist: You're not really convinced you were your father's pet. (*Repeating her statement.*)

Client: Yes. That's what I've been thinking lately. My brother and sister could get away with things, but not me.

Therapist: Uh-huh. It was just a childish prank with them, but when you did anything it was taken more seriously. (*Repeating her statement.*)

Client: (*Thoughtfully, after a silence.*) You know, I had to live up to such high standards. And for so many years. Yet I'm not sure what my standards are. I mean, what *mine* are.

Therapist: Mmm-hmm. Which are deeply yours and which you've been carrying out just to please your parents. (*Clarification.*)

Client: Yes. Yes, that's right. I guess I don't actually have any of my own. When I have to decide something, I just do whatever occurs to me at the moment. But I don't actually *decide*, because I don't know what I think.

Therapist: You're not clear about what you yourself believe in. (*Repeating her statement.*)

Client: Yes. That's right. (*Pause.*) It probably goes back to my family. We had a big family. Somebody always had to keep everybody happy. Well, I was the one. I've always done that outside the family, too, smoothing things over for everybody else, while it *seemed* as if I were having a good time myself.

Therapist: (*Nods.*) You always kept things going nicely for the others. (*Repeating her statement.*)

Client: Yes. But who was I? Who *am* I? I mean, uhh—what do I think inside myself? That's what I don't know. What I think or who I am—I don't know.

Therapist: I see. You feel you have submerged yourself in the needs of everyone else, trying to please them, feeling adequate that way, that you belong; yet you've lost *yourself* while doing it. (*Clarifying and encouraging her to act as she feels.*)

Client: (*Shaking her head sadly.*) I've been going through the motions so that people will like me. But I don't want to do the things I do for them. It's not sincere. I'm not real.

Gestalt Therapy

Gestalt therapy is an existential approach. It stresses what goes on between the therapist and client. Their relationship, its openness and honesty, is most important. The therapist aims at getting the client to take the responsibility for what he is doing *in the present*. Great emphasis is placed on his awareness of his thoughts and feelings and on acting in accord with them. Once aware, the client discovers that the pain involved in changing is less than that involved in remaining the same.

The therapist avoids the exploration of the client's past, *refusing to look for causes*. He sees the discovery of causes as a maneuver to avoid taking responsibility for one's behavior by blaming it on others or on external factors. The Gestalt therapist believes the person changes very little by merely finding out what motivates behavior. Only awareness of what he or she does in the present and how he does it, leads to change. Of course, he must be willing to change.

The therapist offers a very personal face-to-face way of working. He insists that the client avoid any type of impersonal discussion. The client repeats an idea to become aware of just how much or how little he means what he is saying. To assist the client in discovering his attitudes and beliefs, the therapist prods him to state exactly what he is thinking and feeling. The therapist is thus very active. He interprets the client's bodily movements—a smile, hesitation, or change of voice—so the client can increase his awareness of what is going on within him. The therapist may ask him to act out a quality—numbness, excitement, or any other that he feels—to give it a voice and then talk. In this way he tries to tap parts of the client's self of which he ordinarily is only dimly aware.

In dream analysis, the therapist considers the client to be all the parts and persons in his dream. But the client may find himself unable to discover what the dream means, despite the therapist's efforts. The therapist then urges him not to look outward for a clear view but to tolerate the anxiety of being confused until finally he can understand.

Periodically, the therapist reports what his own awareness is. When he cannot do this, he withdraws into himself and searches until he decides what he wants to do next.

Harry, a very verbal man of thirty, having

been in therapy about one year, has recently expressed a desire to stop smoking.

Client: I think I'm doing better with the smoking.

Therapist: You've been able to cut down?

Client: Oh, yes. Since two weeks ago I'm down to half—a pack and a half instead of three.

Therapist: That's pretty good.

Client: Remember you asked me to watch for the times I smoked—what I was doing, what was going on? (*The therapist had urged the client to focus on immediate experiencing.*)

Therapist: Yes.

Client: Was I surprised. I almost never smoke when I'm alone! It's when I'm with people. I'm not comfortable, and it gives me something to do—light up, puff, flick the ashes. I don't have to look at the other person so much. I guess I've always felt inferior, ever since I was a boy. I remember . . . .

Therapist: (*Interrupting.*) Can you take a specific situation you've been in this past week, where you started to smoke because you were not relaxed? (*Bringing the client back to the present.*)

Client: Let's see. Yeah. I went to lunch with Dennis, my boss. We've done that lots of times. But this time he wanted me to meet a guy, Bill Jenkins, from Aerojet. That's one of the companies we contract with. My work goes directly to this guy, and Dennis thought we could work together better if we—oh, exchanged ideas.

Therapist: And you found yourself lighting up?

Client: I sure did! But I was about to light my second one when I remembered what you had suggested. So I stopped, put it back in the pack, and sat there, asking myself, "What am I *feeling* right now?" And you know—I was *afraid*! I stayed with it, and after a while I realized what it was. This Jenkins is a real sharp guy, and I wasn't sure I could hold my own with him, or what Dennis would think.

Therapist: I see.

Client: Well, I just stayed nervous, that's all. I was sweating, and without a cigarette I was very jittery. I didn't like it! I hate to think I have to be either scared or else smoke to hide it.

Therapist: How do you feel right now?

Client: Now? You mean here?

Therapist: Yes.

Client: Oh, I'm all right. I . . . damn! I didn't even know I was smoking. (*He puts out the cigarette.*) (*Pauses.*) I know. I was thinking you would expect me to do that more and more—question it, go without, and be tense.

Therapist: For a while that may be the price of really letting in what your feelings are. (*Encouraging the client to accept the anxiety until he can deal with it effectively.*)

Client: The thing is, once I know what I am thinking, feeling—damn! It seems I'm always so nervous—*afraid*—that's the right word.

Therapist: Afraid of me, too?

Client: Yeah, what you will think of me. I want you to think I'm progressing. My friends think . . . .

Therapist: (*Interrupting.*) What do *you* think? (*Bringing the discussion back to them.*)

Client: I think I am. Like with Dennis and Jenkins—I sat there, hardly listening to them, telling myself "I'm nervous, I'm nervous." Letting it in.

Therapist: And right now?

Client: I'm afraid. I want you to think I am all right.

Therapist: Will you just focus on that feeling now.

Client: (*Repeats.*) I'm afraid. I want you to think I am all right.

Therapist: You're very restless. You have been twisting around in the chair, not knowing what to do with yourself. (*To heighten client's awareness of his feelings.*)

Client: I don't know what you think about how I am handling this smoking thing. What do you think?

Therapist: Seems to me you are doing very well with it

But—there is a feeling I keep getting . . .(*He pauses and searches.*) You *try* to make a good impression on me. You point out things; you cover all the bases; you work awfully hard to put yourself over. But Harry, you're not *real* when you do that. (*Emphasizing being more open with others, as well as between themselves.*)

Client: (*Quietly.*) I know what you mean. I'm always trying to impress you. I wish I could just *be*.

Therapist: (*Smiling.*) You might find out that what you are isn't so bad after all.

Client: (*Smiling too.*) It would be great if I could really feel that.

Existential Therapy

Existential therapy emphasizes self-awareness, concern with the client's subjective experience, and the search within himself rather than the world outside for the meaning of his existence. It focuses on what behavior is and what it means, not what causes it.

The therapist must be open to the client's world if he is to share his anxiety and pain. While he is aware of the client's distorted ways of reacting to him, he does not emphasize these. He may represent parental figures who once were important in the client's life, but the therapist also lets himself be known as a person in his own right. He concentrates on describing the client's emotional moods. He pays little attention to the unconscious, since he can neither observe nor encounter it directly. He accepts as reality whatever the client feels reality is. He explains this reality only in terms of what the client presents to him. *Why* this particular reality exists has more meaning after both client and therapist know *what* it is. The client's unconscious represents the experiences that he does not dare to have. The therapist does *not* focus on the painful events of the client's life. Instead, he looks for the ways in which the client does not allow himself to experience life fully.

As the client becomes aware that he is responsible for himself, he becomes anxious. The therapist helps him de-

velop the capacity to confront this anxiety. Facing the ultimate anxiety—death—is central to existential psychotherapy. Rewording the "to be or not to be" choice, the therapist
proposes "to be *and* not to be." He feels that accepting the
existential anxiety of life is necessary for self-discovery and
growth. He broadens the client's awareness of his resistance
and distortion as he tries to ignore this anxiety. He puts the
goal of becoming as natural and real as possible before comfort in living. So the client must give up his efforts to escape
his limitations; instead, he must accept and change them.
The therapist helps him do this by pointing out how the client maneuvers to evade existential anxiety, succeeding only
in converting it into neurotic anxiety.

*A man of thirty who has been in existential
therapy for one year.*

Client: Sometimes I still wonder why we had that awful
fight. We've been divorced for four years now and I
still wonder. Except for that one time, I was always
nice to her, *always.*

Therapist: Maybe that's why you had the fight. (*Interpreting.*)

Client: (*Pause.*) Because I was holding things in?

Therapist: Because you *chose* to hold things in when there
was something to be ironed out between you. (*Insisting the client take responsibility for his behavior.*)

Client: Uh-huh.

Therapist: For a long time you put a better face on things
than was actually the case.

Client: I always tried to avoid arguments, if that's what you
mean. Was that wrong?

Therapist: It looks that way, doesn't it? You *let* it build up in
you until finally you exploded. For you to beat her, you
must have been terribly angry. You must have held in a
great deal.

Client: I did, I did. I always tried to be nice.

Therapist: Nice? How real could it have been when you
were so angry inside? (*Insisting on honesty.*)

Client: Yes . . .I see.

Therapist: Yet you decided to be "nice" over and over again. Until the fight, when she left you. You always denied the conflict within you, and your anxiety over expressing it. Just as today you deny you still hurt because of the divorce. (*Suggesting he admit his pain.*)

Client: (*Sighing.*) I see now that I had a lot of rottenness in me that I couldn't admit. Oh, that must go way back. We were always taught to avoid arguments and fighting. (*Bitterly.*) I've been "nice" all my life.

Therapist: Maybe it's time to try facing up to things as they happen. (*Suggesting he admit his existential anxiety.*)

Client: Uh-huh, it's just that it seems like inviting trouble to make arguments if they can be avoided.

Therapist: Inviting trouble? (*Imparting insight.*)

Client: Mmmmmmm. I guess the trouble is already there.

Therapist: You invite trouble by being genuine?

Client: But to admit it, to admit things aren't perfect, and accept them that way, not getting upset—that's hard.

Therapist: That's the decision you have to make—to live with your trouble, not to push it under the rug. (*Insisting he accept existential anxiety.*)

Client: Mmmmmmmm-hmmmm.

Therapist: It's when you decide not to that you get into greater trouble. And then you have to take the responsibility on yourself for things going wrong because it's you who have made a false relationship. You can't shove it off on your wife or your mother or whomever it would be today. (*He must take responsibility for what he chooses to do and not avoid it.*)

Client: (*Silence.*) When I think of how I worried about how things were—on the surface, I mean—while actually Linda must have felt so alone—because I wasn't really there—not the real me. What we could have had together. I loved her. (*Tears, his voice breaking.*) I loved her and the baby. (*Pause.*) It all got so mixed up. I can't get used to the idea that it all happened—getting separated. If only I could have been less afraid. (*Under-*

stands that he made things much worse because he could not confront his existential anxiety.)

Group Therapy

There are many types of groups. Some are for married women, others for mothers, single women, adolescent boys, married couples, whole families, and so on. Except for married couples and families, a group usually consists of five to ten clients. In a mixed group, the therapist ordinarily attempts to have an approximately equal number of men and women. The group meets at least once a week for one and one-half to two hours. Some groups meet more often. The members sit so they more or less face one another. A therapist is always present at regular meetings (sometimes they meet informally without him). Some groups employ two therapists. In that case, each therapist stimulates a different type of interaction, one often functioning as a father figure, the other as a mother figure. Many therapists regularly meet individually, too, with members of the group. Others prefer to confine their relationship to the group.

During the first few sessions, the members become aware of the enormous similarity of their problems. The therapist has tried to select the group members so there will be considerable common experience among them. He excludes those who might draw from the group interaction but not contribute to it, as a self-centered or paranoid (suspicious and hostile) person might.

Most clients are self-conscious about discussing their personal problems with strangers. It is hard enough for them to do so with a therapist. But once they have participated in a few group sessions, most settle down to work. The therapist may suggest that each client introduce himself to the group, tell a little about himself, and then indicate the kinds of problems he feels he has. He may ask a client how he feels about the ideas that have been expressed by someone else. Sometimes he goes around the circle, asking each member to express himself in relation to what is happening in the group. Through such simple devices, the members soon become aware of their common problems and goals and realize that they can help each other. Each member becomes more confident and resourceful by experiencing himself as important and helpful to the others.

As group members learn to recognize their common problems, they lose the sense of isolation that blocked them from changing their behavior. They come to feel that they *belong* in the group. They examine the maturity level of how they react to one another when a problem arises. This pinpoints who it is that has the problem. They express their anger with relative freedom, expecting the others to be concerned enough to allow them to do so. Because each member not only seeks help but also tries to provide it to the others, a good deal of the self-centeredness of individual therapy is avoided. This helps the members develop a more balanced picture of themselves, their worth and what they have to offer. Though some members tend to operate on the edge of the group at first, it is not long before they are drawn into the interaction as they accept one another and become more open. And it is helped along because they have many problems in common.

Each member relies on the others to be absolutely honest about how they react to each other. Courtesy, tact, glossing over, and hypocrisy have little place in group therapy. When two members disagree, the group analyzes the personality factors involved. Under the combined influence of the therapist, other group members, and their own probing, the two members usually get to the bottom of it.

Let us look in on a group that has been meeting for three years.

Helen, thirty-four, is tall and slender. Her blue eyes, set in an oval face, light up as she smiles. She projects a very pleasant warmth and interest. She is the kind of woman men find feminine and women frequently envy.

About six months ago she had formed a friendship with another member about her own age, Louise. Their relationship was harmonious at times, stormy at others.

At this group session, Helen burst out with the opinion

that Louise did not really care about her. She was convinced that Louise found nothing likable about her. Louise
became very reassuring. She described her warm feelings
for Helen. She reminded Helen that she had always admired her looks and that she had always wished she had
Helen's taste in home decor and her poise and skill in enter-
taining. No matter what Louise said, however, Helen could
derive no comfort from it. She hung her head, wiped slowly
at her eyes, and her voice fell to a whisper. The entire
group, including Louise, could only feel sorry for her. She
seemed to shrink, becoming a little girl, mutely pleading to
be liked and wanted. Yet Louise, though sorry for her, was
also irritated. Helen's distress implied that Louise must be
an awful person to make anyone as unhappy as Helen was.

The therapist decided to emphasize to the group and to
Helen that they were witnessing a maneuver that was typical of her. He asked her how she had acted in childhood
when her mother scolded her in settling a dispute between
her and her younger sister. Helen had been jealous because
she felt that her mother preferred her sister. Did she talk
back to her mother, get angry or sullen, or did she cry? In
tears, Helen admitted that she cried. Her mother could never endure her tears and in the end would throw her arms
around Helen and tell her how much she loved her.

Various incidents in Helen's life now fell into focus for
the group. First, she had had periods of depression and cry-
ing with her first husband. He exhausted himself trying to
pull her out of them, hating every moment of it. After her
divorce, when she returned to live with her mother, they
had periodic arguments during which Helen would be depressed and weeping. Her mother consoled her, accepting
blame, yet never really knowing for what. More recently, in
Helen's second marriage, the arguments would start out
over some trivial point, then snowball into the typical depressed weeping. And all the while, her husband, feeling
like a brute for upsetting her, would reassure her endlessly.
Now she was doing the same thing with Louise before the
group. Once Helen had started to react in this way, she

could not seem to stop herself. Whatever drove her to these maneuvers to begin with, the weeping seemed to acquire a momentum of its own.

Helen's tyranny was subtle. Through her suffering she pressured the other person to humble himself and assume the blame. And at the same time that she put herself in the right, she indirectly expressed her hostility. Finally, her tears brought forth a display of attention and warmth that she took for love. So, very slowly, she allowed herself to be cajoled into drying her tears and smiling again, though somewhat wanly. She was actually a very dominant woman who ruled with the tender tear rather than the harsh voice or the stubborn will.

Helen had never interacted with the therapist in this particular manner during their individual hours. She now recognized that she had begun these maneuvers on a number of occasions but abandoned them when he had refused to feed her reaction by consoling her and taking blame on himself. In the broader arena of the group, her childish and disruptive pattern emerged clearly. Once exposed, it seemed so repugnant to her that she could no longer use it easily. She saw that she would have to confront an issue on its own merits. She could no longer mistake pity for love. If she wanted to assert herself, she would have to come out from behind her mask of tears and do so openly. Subsequent events showed that she could do this.

Chapter 13

Achieving Our Best Self

Because we become increasingly centered within ourselves as we develop, we can never mingle ourselves with others as fully as we wish. To do so is to sacrifice part of our own identity and to become confused and anxious. These two conflicting needs—to immerse ourselves completely in another, yet to preserve our individuality—culminate in the most painful and dreaded of all experiences: that of feeling alone, denied the love we are trained to seek.

In response to the pain of our aloneness we erect bulwarks against it—bulwarks, unfortunately, that for many are all too fragile. We cultivate the relationships and qualities and activities that rescue us from the abyss of emptiness and absurdity by creating meaning. Then living matters, ceasing to be merely a transient episode.

It is reassuring to realize that, from the earliest days, all our energies (however unknowingly) already are directed toward the creation of meaning. Our socialization, whereby we internalize what those who went before us considered worth transmitting—values, codes, beliefs, morals, ethics—places our feet squarely on the path of seeking meaningfulness.

It may not be a particularly new idea to the reader that the person must feel that life is meaningful if he or she is to find it worth living. But a number of ideas that are related to meaningful living may have been brought into sharper focus by this book.

If it is important to acknowledge that a person often feels very alone in the world, that he can never love anyone as fully as he desires; then it is at least equally important to him that an author describe what the person can do to make life meaningful—seek close relationship, a clear sense of identity, values, existential living, purpose or goals, creative expression, the excitement of intellectual activity, hope, and, for those who can believe, religious faith. It is these that foster a positive outlook on life. Though these factors must be continuously renewed by the person, it is deeply reassuring to him to realize that, substantially, fulfillment lies in his own hands. It removes chance from his life, at least to a considerable extent. It offsets the uncertainty of plodding blindly from one day to the next, with his feet on no sure path. It puts the issue squarely on the person's shoulders—to pursue those qualities and relationships that alone can fill his or her life with meaning.

If the person will strive to tap his dormant potentials, he will discover, often much to his surprise, that he has many resources of which he was unaware. Most people can live so much more fully than they do. Too many have so abandoned the search for a meaningful life that to them it seems more or less normal to live in dull despair. R.D. Laing has expressed this unfortunate condition very well in *The Politics of Experience*:

> The condition of alienation, of being asleep, of being unconscious, . . . is the condition of the normal man . . . . What we think is less than what we know;

what we know is less than what we love; what we love
is so much less than what there is. And to that precise
extent we are so much less than what we are.

Yet, I want to emphasize that people *do* have the power
to make their lives meaningful. The challenge is clear—to
become all that we are: to be deeply touched by others and
to touch them; to place ourselves in the position of being
needed by a partner, child, friend, or parent; to aspire to a
goal of our own choosing; to risk being authentic with others
and with ourselves; to dare to self-actualize, unafraid of cen-
sure from within or without; to value time and above all
things, the gift of life; and to let our anxiety goad us to create meaning in place of nothingness.

Rather than try to create meaning by themselves, many
people could succeed better if they turned to a professional
psychotherapist for help. As a practising therapist, I naturally think in these terms. It might be well, therefore, to discuss some of the questions commonly raised by the prospective client and to lay down some guidelines that will
help him select a therapist for his particular needs.

I use "analytic" in a broad sense to include Freudian,
Adlerian, modified analytic, interpersonal, and many eclectic and existential therapists, all of whom work on a fairly
long-term, deep basis.

I suggest behavior modification as often being very
effective for those with fears (of airplanes, elevators, high
places, small places, highways) and for habit formations
(drinking, smoking, nail biting). Yet, I must qualify this suggestion. Think of a suicidal woman whose fantasied method of ending her life is to jump from a high place. She presents a fear of high places. Clearly, this fear is protective of
her life and should not be removed, even if it could be.
Those who want to know the underlying basis of their pho-
bias might well go to an analytic or long-term therapist. Remember that fears and habit formations are symptoms, and,
as such, are related to the underlying psychological process.

Crisis intervention, a brief number of sessions (perhaps
six to twelve), can often help the person through a crisis

such as the death of a loved one, financial reverse, loss of a job, a broken engagement, divorce, or a physical disability requiring sudden changes.

I think that those with marriage problems can often accomplish more with a therapist than with a "marriage counselor." Those who do not feel it necessary to get to the bottom of things can avail themselves of a marriage counselor or of a group consisting of married couples. Those who are in relationship, but unmarried, can enter individual therapy or group therapy, or both, depending upon their goals.

For those who would like to develop their listening, empathic, communicative skills, their ability to become more expressive of their feelings, their awareness, and to discover how others see them, a psychotherapy group or a sensitivity training group can be very helpful.

A fairly long-term type of therapy is indicated—either eclectic, Rogerian, existential, or analytic—for those with problems of withdrawal, self-concept, guilt, sexual attitudes (sexual behavior is being treated increasingly by behavior modification), dependency, psychosomatic disorders, inability to function existentially, clinging to distant or frustrating relationships, or excessive use of defense mechanisms such as repression, overeating, and depression.

For those who are functioning well but wish to maximize their potentials (this group of clients is increasing rapidly), either an analytic, eclectic, Rogerian, or existential therapist would be a good choice.

I want to emphasize that those who undertake psychotherapy are no less effective in their functioning than those who do not. In fact, the need for therapy by no means always influences a person to undertake it. Until recently psychotherapy has been used primarily to help the person with emotional problems. Its role has been to help him improve functioning to the point where the person could satisfy his own needs and the needs of those importantly associated with him. Today, however, psychotherapy is rapidly being expanded to help those who are already functioning adequately but wish to realize their potentials more fully. I emphasize this because I think this trend will increase in the near future.

As things are now, however, most people undertake therapy because they feel they absolutely need to. Nevertheless, other factors influence the decision—familiarity with the concept of therapy, religious outlook, expectations, and how well the person can accept exposing himself or herself.

The person's symptoms are the *content*, the *what*, of his or her problems. To discover *why* he manifests these particular problems, his psychological process, neurotic or otherwise, needs to be examined. *How* he expresses his drives and satisfies his needs determines the problem that he manifests. Thus, a young woman brought up in a repressive manner (why) may avoid men (what) because she is homosexually oriented (how).

The qualified psychotherapist is readily distinguished from the unqualified; his credentials are available for inspection, and he is usually a member of the local psychiatric or psychological association or is qualified to become a member. This is not to say that all therapists are equal. Nevertheless, people often make referrals to a therapist based on nothing more substantial than playing golf with the therapist, living next door to him, or receiving referrals, in turn, from him. No doubt the best type of referral is that of a friend who has been to a particular therapist, has been helped, and can describe his working methods.

I prefer the type of therapist who regards the person as a *client*, not a patient. Emotional problems and ineffective patterns of interaction interfere with the person's capacity to satisfy his or her needs. He is not mentally ill. He is not a *patient*. In the doctor-patient relationship a person tends to be passive. In general, effective medical treatment does not depend on whether or not the patient is favorably inclined toward the treatment. But if the collaborative effort of therapist and client in psychotherapy is to be successful, the client must be an active participant. He must change himself. The therapist does not change him.

Since psychiatrists are medical doctors, and since clinical psychologists are also called "doctor" because of their PhD degree, clients may reactivate unconscious attitudes toward the doctor-client relationship which properly belong to the doctor-patient relationship. When this occurs it undermines the client's initiative and self-direction. It is the client who carries the responsibility for progress in therapy. Unlike the patient who extends his arm to the medical doctor for a shot, the client in therapy must activate his own dormant resources in order to mature further.

Therapy can properly last as long as it takes the client to reach any realistic goals that he has set for himself. It may take several months of contact with a new client for the therapist to evaluate how long therapy is likely to take. An evaluation can be made only for specific goals. The time required depends on the therapist's skill and the client's capacity to do the work of therapy—to attend sessions regularly, confront himself or herself, and risk changing.

Psychotherapy as a profession has recruited many female therapists. This may pose a problem for the prospective client. Clients of both sexes have their choice of therapists of both sexes. Is one sex more effective than the other for certain clients? Do male and female therapists have different biases, that, in specific instances, may cause them to be more or less effective with male and female clients?

Consider a woman of thirty who has never related to a man—except disastrously. All her life she has been attracted to women but has never yielded to her homosexual inclinations. She brings to a male therapist all the fear and antagonism that she has always felt toward the male; yet she needs to learn that all males are not as exploitive and punitive as she thinks they are. On the other hand, were she to choose a female therapist she could develop a clearer picture of the crystallized female. In the struggle to establish her identity as a female, she wonders which therapist, male or female, can help her most. She might consult a therapist to explore just this question. My own feeling is that she should first work with a female therapist. Then, when she is clearer in her female identity, she should work with a male therapist, assuming she wishes to function heterosexually.

The prospective client may be confused about the therapist's religious background. The Catholic may feel that no one but a Catholic therapist could understand and sympathize with his values and attitudes. The anti-Semitic client may not want to work with a Jewish therapist. The withdrawn, anti-gentile Jew wonders if he can work constructively with a gentile therapist. In general, I cannot support any of these attitudes. A person's need to displace his personal frustrations to a particular group (which is what is involved most of the time) suggests his insecurity and dissatisfaction with himself and those close to him. Sometimes such a person's feelings can be overcome best when, for instance, a Jewish client consults a gentile therapist, or vice versa, provided the client is not too withdrawn for the therapist to establish a good working relationship. If such clients have worked with a therapist of their own faith but have discontinued therapy for a while, they might do well to resume with a therapist of the disliked group.

Sometimes, as a person changes in therapy, her partner, who is not in therapy, may resent her changing. He may try to influence her to discontinue therapy. As a result of her emerging maturity she may make greater demands upon him, especially if she has been too subordinate before. Once she has begun to change, she can no longer interact with him in her former (less mature) ways. He resists her demands because of his insecurity. He rejects the premise that if he kept pace with her they would get along better. Thus, for one partner in a relationship to enter therapy is no guarantee at all of improvement in their interaction. Indeed, more often than not, the gap between them widens when only one of them moves forward. Therapy then becomes a divisive force between them, and I want to emphasize this for the reader. Actually, a person who resists therapy in his partner unconsciously fears that she will outdistance him in personality growth and refuse to key her behavior to their old lifestyle, one which may have favored him greatly. However, in or out of therapy, whenever one person progresses toward maturity more rapidly than the other, they are in danger of drifting apart.

At present, no precise technique for assessing the depth or degree of emotional problems exists. The therapist's impression will be influenced by the extent of the client's anxiety, the persistence of his or her symptoms, the breadth of his life-space, and the level of need-satisfaction on which he functions. He will take the client's age (often, though not necessarily, accompanied by rigidity that makes changing more difficult) into account.

I have discussed certain aspects of psychotherapy at some length in this chapter to encourage those who might be undecided, but on the brink of deciding to seek professional help. Consultation with a specialist in emotional problems and in living is as helpful to the person as is consultation with a lawyer about a legal problem or with a medical doctor about a physical illness. Good luck on your journey into maturity and a meaningful life.

Index